M000111131

Advance Praise for
MentorShift

"Lori Bachman knows mentoring and displays a brilliant knack with a pen as she shares her knowledge. As one who has been the beneficiary of world-class mentors, I can certify that this is a world-class book on mentoring."

— **Norm Augustine, retired Chairman and CEO, Lockheed Martin Corporation**

"*MentorShift* combines a real-life, hands-on process that any leader or medical professional can immediately put to use. The medical community would be greatly served by embracing this book on mentoring."

— **Dr. Latanya Benjamin, Stanford University, School of Medicine**

"Do you want your employees engaged and proactive about sharing knowledge? Buy this book. It will equip your association or agency leaders, managers and employees alike with specific, innovative ways to do just that."

— **Lori Garver, General Manager, Airline Pilots Association; former Deputy Administrator, NASA**

"Mentoring is one of *the* primary methods for inter-generational transfer of vital information. It's been around since the dawn of human tribal societies. Lori Bachman's invaluable *MentorShift* book provides more than ample motivation for becoming a mentor, together with a wealth of suggestions for how to be one with maximum value for both mentor and mentee. It really is a completely comprehensive compilation that enlightens a much discussed but little understood critical aspect of human experience."

— **Rinaldo Brutoco, Founder, World Business Academy**

"Lori Bachman is a dynamite mentor! She understands what it takes to teach individuals and teams how to build their knowledge base and transfer skills in a way that makes them want to jump right in."

— **Ed McCaffrey, former NFL All-Pro wide receiver; three-time Super Bowl champion; co-founder, Dare to Play football camps for children with Down Syndrome**

"Finally! A business book with actionable insights that's full of heart. It gives readers rock-solid specifics that are worth their valuable time, mind and dime. Read it and reap."

— **Sam Horn, author of** *Tongue Fu!*® **and** *POP!*

"There's not one good word to describe *MentorShift*—there are **many**. Straightforward. Conversational. Feeling. Funny. Real. Participatory. Lasting. Finally, there is a book about mentoring that actually shows an understanding of the journey and provides the means to take it—no matter who you are, where you are, or what role you're playing. Lori Bachman is an author who has wisely discerned that mentoring isn't about mentor or mentee, but about both. Always. That keen insight allows this book to deliver on **all** those 'good words' to anyone who reads *MentorShift* and begins the rewarding journey that is mentoring."

— **Larry Robertson, award-winning author of** *A Deliberate Pause;* **founder, the (re) institute and Lighthouse Consulting; former Adjunct Professor of Entrepreneurship, Georgetown University**

Lori Bachman is a true thought leader in the world of mutually beneficial mentoring. Her groundbreaking book, *MentorShift,* outlines a revolutionary shift for companies ready to build a mentoring culture that improves their bottom line and creates lasting cultural change. I intend to recommend it to every executive I know!

— **Denise Brosseau, CEO, Thought Leadership Lab and author of** *Ready to Be a Thought Leader?*

"Mentoring is about education. This book does a fantastic job of getting its readers to ask, 'What do I know that I can teach others and what do others know that I might learn from them?' With Lori's four-step process, the learning baton is passed with finesse."

— **Paul Magelli, Senior Director, Illinois Business Consulting, University of Illinois at Urbana-Champaign**

"Knowledge and experience transfer is a vital part of all emerging and established business organizations. *MentorShift* provides a refreshing perspective on how effective mentoring relationships can have a lasting impact for all involved."

— **Nina Nashif, Founder and CEO, Healthbox**

Mentor
Shift

A Four-Step Process
to Improve
Leadership Development,
Engagement and
Knowledge Transfer

LORI BACHMAN

Copyrighted Material

MentorShift
Copyright © 2014 by MentorWorks Publishing

ALL RIGHTS RESERVED
No part of this publication may be reproduced, stored in a retrieval system or transmitted, in any form or by any means—electronic, mechanical, photocopying, recording or otherwise—without prior written permission, except for the inclusion of brief quotations in a review.

MentorShift® is a registered trademark and as such is protected under the rules and regulations of the U.S. Patent and Trademark Office and the International Trademark Association.

For information about this title or to order other books and/or electronic media, contact the publisher:

MentorWorks
Publishing

MentorWorks Publishing
P.O. Box 630646, Highlands Ranch, CO 80163
www.loribachman.com

Library of Congress Control Number: 2014902657

ISBN: 978-0-9913452-0-5

Printed in the United States of America

Cover and Interior design by: 1106 Design

Publisher's Cataloging-In-Publication Data
(Prepared by The Donohue Group, Inc.)

Bachman, Lori.
    MentorShift : a four-step process to improve leadership development, engagement and knowledge transfer / Lori Bachman.

    pages : illustrations ; cm

    Includes index.
    Issued also as an ebook.
    ISBN: 978-0-9913452-0-5

    1. Mentoring in business. 2. Employees—Coaching of. 3. Organizational learning. 4. Leadership. I. Title. II. Title: Mentor Shift

HF5385 .B33 2014
658.3/124   2014902657

Contents

PART 2: MOBILIZE THE STEPS AND MULTIPLY THE FUTURE

Section 3: Step 1—KNOW. (I Do)

Section 4: Step 2—SHOW. (I Do, You Contribute)

Section 5: Step 3—GROW. (You Do, I Contribute)

This book is dedicated to my parents, Bob and Joan Bachman

Precious and extraordinary mentors throughout a lifetime

Acknowledgments

I BEGIN WITH THANKS TO Sam Horn, my creative writing mentor, strategic thinking partner and friend. She is called the Intrigue Expert® for a reason. She is a genius who helps you communicate what you care about so others get it, value it and act on it.

Thanks to my editing team—Karen Klein, Cheri Grimm, Christina Grimm and Marianne Brousseau for their careful reading of both the big ideas and the small, important details. They kept me steady and on track.

To Jason Clark, my diligent research assistant. His quick, thorough work still amazes me.

I offer thanks to my faithful readers whose honest suggestions helped craft a better manuscript from start to finish—Brenda Abdilla, Sharon Beekmann, Linda Brisnehan, Janice Cappucci, Kelly Condon, Christine Daspro, John Henderson, Jim Kemp, Michael Kemp, Ron Remy and Carrie Sawyer.

A special nod to those who offered me their time and insights through interviews on what mentoring means in their work and lives—Ginger DeReus, Randy Emelo, the late Hanka Kent, Karen Main, Lily Nie, Steve Nordmark, Richard Sherlock, Jack Torpey, Randy Wilhelm, Pat Wilson, Amy Zhong.

To my friends and mentors who knew my passion for this book and dedicated themselves to my writing progress. They cheered me on and picked me up when I needed a lift—Robert Dalal, Susan Sharpe, Marcia Kent, Mary LoVerde and Mark Sanborn.

Thanks to my friends, and former pastors, Dr. Greg and Donna Carlson and Dave Arch, who taught me these powerful MentorShift steps long before I named them so. They instilled in me that mentoring has to multiply to truly last.

I'm grateful to my dear parents, Joan and Bob Bachman, who have mentored me with unfailing wisdom, patience and love through the years. I learned what real mentoring is about from you.

And finally, to the bright sunshine in my life, Annie and Andrew, who lift my spirit each and every day. I'm so proud to be your mom...and yes, I'm done writing, at least for a while!

Foreword

THIS IS A BUSINESS BOOK, but make no mistake, it will make you think deeply, imagine greatly and laugh freely.

When I read *MentorShift—A Four-Step Process to Improve Leadership Development, Engagement and Knowledge Transfer* by Lori Bachman, I knew immediately that I'd found a needed book. Lori has crafted all of the right elements—sound guidance and solutions, inspiration and wit—into a mentoring system that will provide a *strategic ROI for your business, employees and a personal win for you.*

Are you like me and you've had a work mentoring experience that wasn't quite what you hoped for? This book will change that.

MentorShift's message says that mentoring in our business is not working and needs reworking, in fact it needs a SHIFT...A 7.5 on the Richter scale kind of shift. There are far too many unguided, unfinished or unfulfilling mentoring relationships that don't produce the results they could.

This book prepares you to make that all-important shift by showing you how to:

- Remove excuses that hold you back from a successful mentoring relationship
- Find or be the right kind of mentor
- Effectively equip an individual to mentor someone else

In the Introduction to the book, Lori shares the premise of this book. She says,

> "First, you and I want to make a difference in our lives; change something, help someone, know that we matter. We are hard-wired that way and there's no getting out of it.

Second, if we are intentional and creative, we can do just that and nothing can stop us."

I agree with her. You and I want to create meaningful, mutually rewarding relationships with others and sometimes aren't exactly sure how best to do it.

You notice that I've used the word "equip" a moment ago. Perhaps what I like best about *MentorShift* is just that—it is a book about equipping. It equips and prepares you with techniques you can use *right now* to get the most from the time you invest in teaching and learning from others.

I promise you that if you follow Lori Bachman's advice on how to transfer work and life skills, wisdom and knowledge through her four-step *MentorShift* process, you will realize a profound and lasting way to make a difference.

And your company will thank you too as it reaps the benefits of improved morale, productivity and profitability.

I urge you to incorporate *MentorShift* principles into your life—a sure and steady way to make the world and your world a little bit better.

— MARK SANBORN
Author of *The Fred Factor* and
You Don't Need a Title to Be a Leader

Introduction

WHAT DO YOU GET WHEN you cross a former Fortune 100 aerospace executive with a cowboy's daughter and a woman on a mentoring mission?

That question is a peek at my introduction to you. I hope it begins to answer: "Who is this person and why is she writing this book?"

Woman on a Mentoring Mission

I *am* a woman on a mission.

I've learned a powerful, lasting way to mentor and I've made it my mission to show you how to do it, too. I'm eager to do this because I believe a couple of timeless truths about people and life.

First, you and I want to make a difference in our lives, change something, help someone, know that we matter. We are hard-wired that way and there's no getting out of it.

Second, if we are intentional and creative, we can do just that and nothing can stop us.

Many months ago, full of this passion and as the brew of this book was percolating in my brain, I logged on to my computer early one morning and opened up today's news. I was greeted with several skirmishes in the Middle East, an alarming drop in the overseas stock markets, summer storms pounding the eastern seaboard and my favorite television program hitting the skids.

As I nursed my cup of dark, roasted blend, I reflected, "And there's not a thing I can do about any of it."

I am definitely a glass-half-full kind of person so this reflection was in no way philosophical lamenting or cosmic complaining. It was just a statement of fact.

That realization led me down a more ponderous path, though, to ask the question, "What *can* I really control? What can any of us really control?"

And despite the early hour and before the caffeine had done its job, I instantly recalled what I'd learned many times over.

I can mentor.

And here's the good news. So can you.

Every morning, despite what the early news offers up to welcome you to the day, despite the ups and downs in the world faraway or in your backyard or your cubicle, you can decide to make a difference by mentoring someone else.

Or if you're not quite there yet, you can decide to have someone mentor you.

That's the first reason for my mentoring mission. The decision to be in a mentoring relationship is one thing you can control every day from now forward. There's power and responsibility and freedom in that fact.

There's a second reason.

Throughout my years as an aerospace executive and in my consulting career since then, I have looked deeply into the business world and observed how businesses let mentoring happen. I've seen that the model is often ineffective and I know it can be fixed.

Think about your workplace mentoring experience up until now. Does it look anything like what I observed?

- Your company has paired you up with a mentor (mentor matchmaking, if you will!) and each month you sit dutifully across the desk from them—stapled, hammered or glued to your chair, never budging an inch. Talk, talk and more talk. *Zzzzzz.*
- Your mentor waxes lyrical about what he did "back when he was a pup" or "what the company was like 20 years ago when she was hired on."
- When the hour is over, you are sent packing 'til the third Tuesday of next month. You walk out not knowing much more than when you walked in.
- You give up and resort to hanging over your cubicle wall, begging the kindness of a fellow worker to help you learn how the new system works.

- Despite the unfulfilling proposition above, you (and your company) can "check the box" on the mentoring tally sheet but you gained little or no real-world skills that position you for advancement and contribution.

Sound familiar? If so, you'd agree that the mentoring model in most workplaces needs some dramatic repair.

I think it needs more than a repair; I think it needs a SHIFT. A 7.5 on the Richter scale kind of shift.

Did you know U.S. organizations spent approximately $164 billion on employee training and development in 2013 with much of that money spent on outside consultants and training specialists?[1]

Are they getting their money's worth? Why aren't companies tapping their internal human capital instead?

Companies are wasting resources! They are leaving billions on the table by not leveraging their human resource talent more effectively. A lot of opportunities (and talented employees) are falling through the cracks.

Two up-and-coming colleagues of mine, Max and Lauren, drove this point home for me. Both are professionals I truly admire: Innovative and ambitious with potential to head to the top. I asked each of them, "Who has mentored you along the way?"

Max, bright, articulate and in his mid-thirties, furrowed his brow and said, "Well, just let me think a minute; I don't know if you would call this person a mentor, although my company matched us up. He just had me show up at his office every couple of months and we'd talk, or I should say, he would talk. I honestly didn't get much out of it."

Lauren, an energetic software whiz in her late twenties, flat out said, "I don't think I've had a mentor, not a real one."

In Max's mentoring relationship, he had been bored and left wanting. Lauren just knew that no mentor's face popped into her mind.

How can this be? These are sharp individuals who are going to make a real impact in their worlds. Yet neither had clear-cut, "leap to your mind" mentors who had come alongside and invited them into the fray.

My mission is never to see another Max or Lauren—employees who can't describe an unforgettable mentoring experience. Never.

Read on, and you will learn about the powerful MentorShift process this book describes. My mentees know it because I've shown them.

When I led a finance leadership development program, team members would frequently say, "Write this mentoring stuff down! People need to know there's a different way to mentor."

And thus *MentorShift* took its first full breath.

Executive and Business Leader

As a former executive with Lockheed Martin Corporation and current consultant to numerous other businesses, my professional life has been filled with meetings, spreadsheets and airline reward programs in abundance through the years. Like my colleagues, I've looked forward to my weekly paycheck, grumbled over maddening bosses and celebrated a happy hour or two.

I've suited up in my designer pinstripes and painful pointy-toed shoes for tough presentations to top-level business and government leaders. I've labored into the wee hours while swilling down high-octane caffeine drinks guaranteed to bring home an on-time project.

I've seen millions of dollars earned and lost, and volatile company stock prices weaken the knees of the most stalwart leaders.

I've exulted when my team closed a multi-billion-dollar merger and felt bereft when other deals in which we'd invested our very hearts and souls did not come to pass (though many times that was the optimum outcome).

I have lived the three-word sacred mantra of the workplace: Maximize shareholder value.

I've been there and done that and am proud to say I've been a committed creature in the world of commerce.

I spent many of those eventful commerce years in the aerospace industry.

When my children were young, as they considered my time at "the rocket factory," they would ask me, "What's it like to hang out with astronauts?" I would smile at that question and answer, "Of course, it's beyond cool." (Who wouldn't like working with men and women who have "slipped the surly bonds of earth and danced the skies on laughter-silvered wings?"[2])

"And not only that," I'd continue, "there are many brilliant people who make it possible for the astronauts to fly. I get to work with them too."

I will forever brag about my colleagues who designed spacecraft to see Venus' landscape through its clouds, built rovers to crawl across Martian terrain and fashioned satellites to snatch stardust from a passing comet's blaze.

Every time I look up in the evening sky and see the moon, Venus or Jupiter, luminous, winking back at me, I smile. I say to myself, "They seem like old friends, we've been there."

I lived and loved that world for many years and still do.

Cowboy's Daughter

I can't leave this introduction without letting you know about an equally powerful force in developing my mentoring passion.

From the heartland of cattle country to the far reaches of deep space, my journey unfolds. I grew up in Grand Island and Omaha, Nebraska and although my travels have taken me from Manhattan to Moscow, and Beijing to Burbank, there's still nothing like heading back to where the land is flatter than a buckwheat pancake and "the corn grows as high as an elephant's eye."

Careful, I might start singing.

My dad and grandpa were experts in the ranching and cattle business. Through their example, I picked up some wholesome values, appreciation of hard work and insight into business impacts you can't control—markets, commodity prices and how much rain falls from the sky.

I found out that de-tasseling corn for a summer job was an interesting preparation for life in the corporate mergers and acquisitions world. How else would I have known that sometimes what you throw away adds more value to the product than if you'd kept it. (The corn's tassel is thrown away, for those without an agricultural bent.)

I learned from my grandpa that if you are driving by a feedlot and you inhale deeply "it smells like money." Bet you didn't know that!

And I saw what real mentors were all about—people who are *the real deal*.

The rural Midwest was a great place to grow up. Shoveling...well, I should say, "helping out" in the ranch corrals and watching Dad and Grandpa live a life tied to the earth will forever shape my perspective. Now I am a bona fide city girl but lessons I learned there speak to a business world today.

Answering the *MentorShift* Call

I've kept my ear to the ground about mentoring for many years. As I've listened to you, my fellow mentors and mentees, I knew *MentorShift* had to address a couple of key issues and answer the underlying questions.

First, there are obstacles that hold you back from finding and being the kind of mentor you would like to be.
How can those obstacles be resolved?

Second, you would find it easier to do the whole wonderful mentoring thing if there was a discernible path to follow.
What would that path look like?

I have organized the book to address those two questions.

Part 1, "Motivate Your Mentoring Relationship" provides a foundation for you to examine your attitudes about mentoring, the roadblocks you might have and then discover ways to seek, find and become a great mentor.

Part 2, "Mobilize the Steps and Multiply the Future" offers you a straightforward, effective four-step path to take you from mentee…to mentor…to multiplying mentor.

It's with this direction and from these rich and varied life experiences that *MentorShift* shouted out to be shared with you.

Are you ready?

Let's start mentoring!

Lori Bachman
Denver, Colorado

PART 1

Motivate Your Mentoring Relationship

Bravo, Mr. Jobs, We *Can* Put a Ding in the Universe— Wired to Do Something that Matters

"I just want to do something that matters. Or be something that matters. I just want to matter."

— JOHN GREEN, NEW YORK TIMES BEST-SELLING AUTHOR

PERHAPS IT'S MY EGO, perhaps it's a fear of being a forgotten wisp in the wind, but either way, I have never related to the poem, *The Indispensable Man*. The verse reflects,

> "Sometime when you feel that your going
> Would leave an unfillable hole,
> Just follow these simple instructions
> And see how they humble your soul;
>
> Take a bucket and fill it with water,
> Put your hand in it up to the wrist,
> Pull it out and the hole that's remaining
> Is a measure of how you will be missed.[3]

I've always had a puzzled reaction to this idea. Really? There's nothing there after I'm gone and the hole just fills back up?

May it never be!

Steve Jobs didn't entertain the thought of letting the hole fill up behind him either. In fact, he often expressed, "I want to put a ding in the universe."

Like Mr. Jobs, don't we all want to put our own ding, our own impression, in the world around us?

I never walk into a McDonald's without thinking about my own legacy. No, the tempting aroma of French fries doesn't spur me to existential wanderings. It seems like a funny association but it makes sense when you know the story.

One of my favorite books is Jim Paluch's *Leaving a Legacy—An Inspirational Guide to Taking Action and Making a Difference*. It's a story about seven cantankerous, elderly men who meet each morning at a McDonald's restaurant to lament how boring and pointless their lives are. They call themselves "The Board of Directors."

After an unexpected wake-up call, they change The Board's purpose from that of a miserable pity party to gathering up all of their accumulated years of wisdom and using it to touch the lives of others. Each man shares his own unique piece of wisdom and helps someone else in his own lasting way.

I was inspired by the story's message that it's never too late to:

- Impart wisdom
- Take action
- Make a difference

Many years ago, like the "board of directors," I received that wake-up call.

For a decade I'd spent what seemed like a lifetime of hours at 35,000 feet, zigzagging back and forth across the country from meeting to meeting in pursuit of my dream.

What was that enticing dream?

I could see it in my mind's eye from early in my career. It was a gold nameplate with a name embossed on it—my own, of course—reading "senior vice president." I imagined the office, the mahogany furniture and panoramic view all the while drowning in stock options galore. It had seemed so important for such a long time.

In pursuit of that goal, I'd reached a point where I was traveling so much and racing so fast that I'd lost all balance in my life. Five cities in a week? No big deal for this kid.

At that time, I had been recruited to write the business plan for a project that was a highly visible undertaking in the space world. The *VentureStar* concept was to ultimately deliver a commercial, privately financed, reusable space plane as a replacement for NASA's Space Shuttle, complete with state-of-the-art design, engines, materials, and at a fraction of the cost. Its charter was to take cargo to the International Space Station, launch satellites and eventually carry passengers like you and me to low-earth orbit.

A lot of hype surrounded the project and it was a daily challenge when I considered the personal energy and commitment required of my team and me, not to mention the expected visibility to the highest levels of government and industry. I presented regularly to the CEOs of major aerospace corporations, conferred with the NASA Administrator, visited investment banks on Wall Street to raise private financing for the venture and engaged with Senate sub-committee members and staffers on Capitol Hill.

With this kind of undertaking, you can understand why the flight attendants knew me by name and often offered me a bottle of wine as I exited the plane. They knew a potential million-miler when they saw one. I dutifully ran to catch my weekly flights out of Denver to Washington, D.C...and everywhere else.

As I would sprint from one connecting flight to another, on occasion, a still, small voice inside of me would nudge me by asking, "What are you running *from* and what are you running *to?*"

I would silence that voice and bury it deep. After all, I was in a job most people would give their eyeteeth to have and meeting people who were the demi-gods in my slice of the business world.

Many months into the project and well into my life as a road warrior, on one business trip, I awakened in my hotel room in the middle of the night, disoriented and scared. I had no earthly idea what city I was in or what day it was (it *had* been five cities that week).

My heart was pounding. I stumbled through the dark to the desk blotter, flipped on the light and looked at the *Welcome* magazine to discover which city I was in and gain my bearings.

I knew something had to give.

As I traveled to the airport at 6 a.m. a week later, bound for my Los Angeles office, I was overcome with tears and emotion. I had hit the wall and knew I had to finally answer that still, small voice. To this day, I call it my "drive with destiny."

As I'd scrambled for the gold nameplate, I hadn't accomplished most of the things that I really wanted to in my life, not the real things, and I'd strayed far from the person I wanted to be.

Humbled yet determined, I promised myself that morning that during whatever time my 5'7" frame had left to inhabit this planet, I would rededicate my life to things that lasted.

I would make mentoring the story of my life.

That same day when I arrived in Los Angeles, I asked my boss, Jerry, for a career discussion, one I knew would be a difficult one to have. I was excited about my decision to make some changes but I was also nervous about the consequences it could bring.

Jerry had seen some of my burnout so he wasn't altogether surprised by my choice. We had a heart-to-heart talk about what I would be leaving on the table and what might be at the other end of my decision. We worked out a plan where I could still support the project until I could smoothly transition my responsibilities to someone else. A few weeks later, I headed back to my home office in Denver.

With years of career runway still ahead, I made some different and life-changing commitments. I still cared deeply about contributing to my workplace in a meaningful way and, at the same time, I integrated some new things alongside that passion: time with family, time to create and time to mentor. I chose to exchange the quest for a gold SVP nameplate for other kinds of treasure.

After that decision point, I continued a rewarding career for over a decade as a financial director specializing in mergers and acquisitions. Three years ago, I chose to take an early retirement from corporate life to start my own company, The MentorShift Group. Each day I'm delighted to serve business teams by equipping them to mentor in a way that creates lasting change.

That's been my journey thus far.

What about *you?*

Have you had your "drive with destiny?"

That moment can be a hard experience, can't it? Hard because you may see, as I did, that those coveted expeditions to faraway places, the do-or-die meetings, the "I'll breathe my last if I don't make it to that networking event" approach can become all about an intoxicating call—to your own ascension in the business world.

What is that intoxicating call for you? Perhaps long hours in the office? Is it the idea that a high-level career slot will bring you the self-esteem and place in this world that you desire?

Philosopher William James said, "The greatest use of life is to spend it for something that will outlast it."[4] Take some time to do a private accounting of what those "things that will outlast" might be for you.

I'm hoping mentoring others will be near the top of the list.

It may seem a million miles down the road, but you may sit one day at the McDonald's with your own board of directors.

What will your story be?

Do something that matters with your career—and with your life. Grab ahold of someone who could use your guidance and mentor them. Mentoring allows you to make a ding, or better yet, a big, crunched-in lasting dent in the universe.

You can be the lucky one to impart wisdom, take action and make a difference.

 ## Questions to Motivate MentorShift

1. Was there any element of my story that you could relate to? If so, what and why?

2. What does your view of life's success look like? Are you satisfied with it or does it need some adjustment? If so, where and how?

3. Who is someone that impresses you with the "doing something that matters" quality of their life?

Prepare for MentorShift—
Resolve Your Mentor Tension

"Avoidance is a wonderful therapy."

— MAGGIE STIEFVATER, AUTHOR

CHAPTER 2

Why Mentoring?— What's In It For ME?

"Successful people are always looking for opportunities to help others. Unsuccessful people are always asking, 'What's in it for me?'"

— BRIAN TRACY, BESTSELLING AUTHOR AND SUCCESS EXPERT

HMMM. IF YOU WANT TO BE successful, be sure to ask "What's in it for them?" as much as you ask, "What's in it for me?"

Perhaps it's a bit hard to do that. After all, we're human. Who doesn't like to make a buck, get ahead and grab ahold of the big brass ring? And when it comes to spending time in a mentoring relationship, we're going to have to be sure there are some personal payoffs.

Fair enough.

There are several reasons you might choose to bypass a mentoring relationship, either as mentor or mentee, and you'll have an opportunity to examine those reasons in detail soon. But before you go there, it might be helpful to set the stage with a definition of mentoring and its benefits.

Definition

I own a vast collection of books about mentoring. In my cozy home library, dozens of these tomes stack casually against one another, leaning on each other like old friends. Each offers a path to a better and more effective way of mentoring. Each describes mentoring and its benefits in a way that provocatively pokes at those offered by the books that lay next to it.

The definitions of "mentor" within those books are good. Many cite a dictionary definition: 1. A mentor is someone who teaches or gives help and advice to a less experienced and often younger person. 2. A mentor is a trusted guide or counselor.[5]

I concur with this description with the caveat that I don't believe the mentee has to be a younger person. It's a welcome experience to be mentored by an individual shorter in years but longer in capability in a given subject or skill.

I do have a favorite definition of mentoring I've rendered that was born out of a lecture series presented by a longtime mentor and colleague, Dr. Gregory Carlson, professor at Trinity International University. The definition touches the significant elements of mentoring and has served mentors and mentees well through the years.

> *Mentoring is a **process** of **mutually sharing your life** with a **chosen person** on a **consistent basis** with the **goal of building them towards maturity in a desired area** and **equipping them to reproduce that process** in someone else.*

The heart of that description beats throughout every page of *MentorShift*. Let's break it down to better appreciate it because it underscores all you will read from this point forward.

What is mentoring?

- *Process – It's a series of actions over time to achieve a result. How long? It might be three months, one year or several decades; in any event it won't be accomplished overnight.*

- *Mutually sharing your life – It's exchanging life experiences in a safe and reciprocal manner.*

- *Chosen person – It's important whom you choose to mentor or be mentored by. It's a deliberate and thoughtful selection.*

- *Consistent basis – It's reliable and consistent get-togethers. When you say you will be there, you show up.*

- ***Goal of building them to maturity in a desired area** – It's helping a mentee to achieve improved skills in their desired area(s).*

- ***Equipping them to reproduce that process** – It's demonstrating a practice that teaches a mentee how to teach others.*

Benefits

That's a good, working definition, isn't it? Now for your next inevitable question—What are the benefits of mentoring to me?

Whether it's from your personal mentoring library or a quick Google search of the "Benefits of Mentoring," the results come fast and furious and they are remarkably similar across the sources.

Benefits from the company viewpoint:

- Improved productivity
- Reduced turnover costs
- Increased retention
- Sustained knowledge sharing

Benefits from the individual's viewpoint:

- Expanded network
- Focused goals
- Shared expertise
- Useful feedback

This abbreviated listing depicts real benefits but you already knew about them and they might be only hackneyed words bouncing around in your gray matter. You're not inspired yet.

There is a bigger benefit to a mentoring relationship.

Leadership expert Anthony Robbins said, "Life is a gift, and it offers us the privilege, the opportunity and the responsibility to give something back by becoming more."

The phrase "the privilege, the opportunity and responsibility" really catches me and I will translate it into my charge to you.

Here is the bold idea about mentoring for you to consider and it carries with it one of the best and brightest benefits of mentoring:

You have a responsibility to mentor and be mentored.

The highest privilege and calling of being human is that of passing on life skills for others' good.

It is the honorable thing to do.

The benefit?

The satisfaction you will receive from doing the right thing.

Remember in the book's Introduction when I shared that mentoring is one thing in this world that you can control? Each day, when you roll out of bed and your feet hit the floor, you can choose to pass on your life skills for the good of another person.

It's a responsibility, an opportunity and a privilege.

And that's what's in it for you.

For now, let's do first things first. We'll come down from the grand call of mentoring and take some time to examine other facts that are just as real. These are the reasons, excuses and objections—call them what you will—that hold you back from experiencing a good mentoring relationship.

There's a tension that must be resolved.

CHAPTER 3

Nothing to Fear but Fear Itself— And Maybe Mentoring

"Don't let the fear of striking out hold you back."

— BABE RUTH, BASEBALL GREAT

YOU ARE WALKING NONCHALANTLY down the hall at work minding your own sweet business. From the corner of your eye you see the quick movement of another figure moving toward you with purpose.

Surprisingly, your inner fight or flight mechanism kicks in full throttle. Who is this person and why is your heart racing? The form and the stride are familiar, the gleam in her eye you recognize well.

It's the boss.

She had mentioned something about a mentoring "opportunity" for you the other day; is she in hot pursuit about that?

Your pulse quickens as you search the hallway from side to side looking for escape. You spy the women's restroom only 20 yards away. You beeline straight for the door, burst into the women's room and slam the stall door shut.

Your chest is pounding—safe at last.

But are you? The restroom door swings open.

"Hello, are you in there?" she cheerily calls out.

"No one here except the cleaning staff, we're just finishing up this stall," you weakly reply.

"Really?" she says, hesitating briefly. "Oh dear, you are such a joker! I'm so glad I caught you. I want to continue our discussion about you becoming a mentor."

You quickly assess your options. There is a small window above—no, you might slip on the porcelain on the way up.

Inside your resolve weakens.

You take a deep breath and tentatively open the stall door. No longer trapped like a wolverine, you step into the light of the restroom. You raise the white flag of surrender.

"Oh, good to see you. I didn't notice you in the hall," you say guiltily.

"I'm so glad we could connect!" she says. "Come by my office when you have a moment and let's discuss the mentoring opportunity I spoke to you about the other day. I'm so excited about this prospect for you, it will be so much *fun* for you to take that next leadership step."

"Are you sure that was me?" You pause momentarily, the white flag waving high. "Oh yes, I vaguely remember that conversation. I can come by later this afternoon."

You both leave the restroom as you mutter, "She has an odd definition of fun."

※   ※   ※

Can you relate to the flight of the mentor-to-be?

Maybe you haven't resorted to hiding in the restroom stall but you've definitely kept your head under the radar when the boss asked for mentor volunteers.

But wait. None of you who are cool, hard-wired, results-driven professionals would ever have a little bit of self-doubt about a little old thing like mentoring, would you?

Of course you wouldn't.

But great news! Just in case you might know someone in *another* department, *down* the hall, who you totally *don't* hang out with, who is not *quite sure* they would know *what to do* to mentor someone else, you can give this whole upcoming section to them.

Or maybe that same colleague hesitates to mentor, not because they lack confidence, but because they are so darn busy they can't see straight, and they are already up to their eyeballs in assignments and action items.

Or maybe they just aren't that interested.

I bet there are a lot of excuses not to mentor.

I love a good challenge, don't you?

Questions to Motivate MentorShift

1. What are the top three excuses you hear in your workplace for why people don't mentor?

2. What are a few reasons you might have for not being in a mentoring relationship?

3. When someone feels they lack confidence to enter a mentoring relationship, what have you seen them do to overcome that?

CHAPTER 4

The Mentor Tension— Newton is Right: Every [Good] Action has an Equal and Opposite Reaction

"Every creative person…faces resistance when they are trying to create something good…The harder the resistance, the more important the task must be."

— DONALD MILLER, AUTHOR

I WANT TO MENTOR… but I don't want to mentor.

I will mentor.

No, I won't mentor.

This is a curious tension, isn't it?

It's a great example of Newton's Third Law, The Law of Motion: For every action there is an equal and opposite reaction.

If you sit down on a chair, your body pushes a force downward and that chair needs to push an equal force upward or the chair will collapse. A rocket taking off from earth propels fuel in one direction and the rocket in the other.

You want to mentor because there are so many fantastic benefits from doing it. You don't want to mentor and you have a list as long as your arm as to why you don't.

You intrinsically know that mentoring is in your nature and best interest. But when the opportunity presents itself, you often want to stand back so you can keep your boots spiffy and clean.

For every reason to mentor, there is a perfectly good excuse not to.

Shine a spotlight on these next two statements, because resolving your mentoring tension is your first important move! I believe these two things from the top of my head down to the tips of my toes.

1. You are naturally, unequivocally, unalterably, innately and inescapably wired to want to mentor and be mentored. (I know, you might not be a believer now but let's check back at book's end.)

2. If you can break through the frequently given excuses to avoid a mentoring relationship provided below (one or two may be particularly near and dear to your heart) then you can embark on a four-step process of mentoring that will change you and others forever.

In order to get to the bottom of the mentoring tension dilemma and because I have such confidence in the above stated beliefs, I queried dozens of colleagues across different walks of life and asked them two simple questions.

Why would you *not* want to be a mentor?

Why would you *not* want to be a mentee?

You won't be surprised by some of their responses because they likely reflect some of your own.

Take note—with each one there is a worthwhile question that might underlie the excuse and that deserves your attention.

1. "Mentoring is a good thing to do, I just don't have the time." (Can I handle it with my other work and family obligations?)

2. "Yeah right. It's just another 'check the box' on my annual review." (Will it be value-added?)

3. "I might get stuck with someone who's a bad fit." (How do I get out of it if it's uncomfortable for me?)

4. "I'm not sure I want someone following me around all the time." (What if my mentee sees me mess up?)

5. "I don't know exactly what to say." (What if it's obvious I haven't mentored anyone before?)

6. "I don't want to have to leave my office to go mentor someone." (What if I have to be become energized and leave the comfort zone of my office?)

7. "There's no way my management will support it." (What if I can't persuade my management to support it?)

The next few chapters address each of the excuses given above. Each offers a story and solutions for you to consider. It's important to honestly deal with the ones you often use so that you are best prepared to walk through the MentorShift steps in Part 2.

"The Seven Too Bs or Not Too Bs"
1. Too Busy—2,051 E-mails and Counting
2. Too Boondoggled—Just Another "Check the Box"
3. Too Binding—If the Shoe Doesn't Fit, Can I Quit?
4. Too Bonding—Transparency Does Not Mean Oversharing
5. Too Baffling—Much Experience, None in Mentoring
6. Too Bottomed Out—Stuck to Your Chairs? Mentees, Beware!
7. Too Blocked—If at First You Don't Succeed…Bail?

Before we delve more into these excuses that can come from either party in the mentoring relationship, there is one important note before we move on. At this point, you may be asking:

"Is this book written for mentors or mentees?"

My answer is—**"YES!"**

Mentees: This book is for you, whether you are a brand-new mentee looking for a first-time mentor…or you're looking for your *next* mentor.

Mentors: This book's for you if you're ready to become a first-time mentor…or you are ready to become a mentor *again*.

I've written the book including both because of a couple of "fall on my sword" convictions I hold about mentoring.

1. *The ultimate goal is to wear two hats—always. You're a mentor. You're a mentee.* When I'm asked, "How do you write a book that addresses two audiences?" I simply answer, "Because the goal is that my readers will eventually, simultaneously be *both* mentor and mentee. Stretching one hand forward…reaching one

hand back." (It makes sense in other ways too; you're a boss and a subordinate, a parent and a child, a teacher and a student—at the same time.)

2. ***The best mentoring relationships happen when it is truly collaboration.*** You will find the finest use of this book if mentor and mentee walk through its process jointly so I've included relevant questions at each chapter's end to provoke thought and guide your discussion. Whether you work in a large corporation, small business or a non-profit organization, you can use MentorShift principles described in this book to build an effective mentoring plan *together.*

So, mentor and mentee, let's look further at these excuses, the real thinking behind them, and a way to bust through.

 ## Questions to Motivate MentorShift

1. What are a couple of these excuses that you can relate to? Why?

2. Do you have an example of a time when you were asked to mentor and you declined? If so, why?

3. In your workplace, if you mentor others, how are you regarded? Does it favorably impact your performance rating?

CHAPTER 5

Too Busy— 2,051 E-mails and Counting

"It's easy to say 'No' when there's a deeper 'Yes' burning inside."
— DR. STEPHEN COVEY, BUSINESS EDUCATOR

STORY

Who is the busiest person you know?

If you could follow that person around all day, would you be impressed with their prodigious feats of efficiency? Would they seem like virtual machines with their ability to plan, process, prognosticate and produce?

Or would you watch in disbelief all day as they dove headlong into a bottomless pool of emails, phone calls, meetings and 5-hour energy drinks—coming up for air only to sprint to their car and text their way out of the parking lot?

When you think of that busy person—is it Mike or Mara down the hall? Or is it you?

We are all busy. Maybe it's why they call what we do "business."

At some level, I get that. I mean, didn't you have 492 hours of unpaid overtime last year? Goodness knows you still didn't get everything done.

But there's a limit. And there's a decision to be made about how busy you choose to be.

Dr. Stephen Covey's book, *Seven Habits of Highly Effective People,* profoundly changed how I saw "busy-ness" in my life.

Dr. Covey, in the chapter "Put First Things First," addresses time management. As he speaks to the urgent, pressing (and oftentimes unimportant) matters that weigh upon us daily, he offers:

"You have to decide what your highest priorities are and have the courage—pleasantly, smilingly, non-apologetically—to say 'no' to [certain] things. And the way you do that is by having a bigger 'yes' burning inside. The enemy of the 'best' is often the 'good.'"[6]

I began to define and commit to that deeper, brighter "yes" burning inside of me.

Here's how I got there—

- I wrote a mission statement for my life.
  - It's simple—an 11-year-old could understand it.
  - It's one sentence long.
  - It's mine and only mine.
  - You can put it on my tombstone someday because it will reflect the person I have sought to be.

- I wrote lifetime goals.
  - I categorized them by family, spiritual, education, physical and financial.
  - Most of them start with "I will be known as a woman who..."
  - They are the "to be" goals that show what I want to be when I grow up.
  - They also have some grand plans that include my bucket list of things yet to accomplish.

- I write yearly goals that carry me to my lifetime goals. They are the measurable steps that march me each year towards living the life I intend to live.

Do you know what the great thing is about having a set-up like this?

Each time I'm approached with an opportunity, a request or an invitation, I filter it through the grid of my bigger "yes." Does this opportunity get me to where I want to go? Does it detract or support?

"I am a woman who is committed to a life of mentoring others and being mentored." That's part of my bigger "yes."

Because you're reading this book, I'm guessing it is part of yours too.

SUGGESTIONS TO SOLVE THE "TOO BUSY" DILEMMA

I understand that we all can legitimately be too busy at a point in time to be in a mentoring relationship. It's extremely important to acknowledge and honor those times.

You might have a season of life where you would be doing an injustice to both you and a mentee if you engaged. Maybe you have an enormous project with an incredibly tight deadline. Perhaps you have a family situation requiring your time and attention.

Honor the reason for that season in your life.

Here's a challenge for you. If you hear yourself saying repeatedly, "I'm sorry, I'm just too tied up right now to mentor someone," I have some questions for you to consider.

The next time you respond, "Not this time, maybe next" ask yourself:

- How often do I hear myself saying that?
- What does this say about how I'm managing my time?
- When I am busy, am I doing things that engage my mind and lift my spirit?
- Is this an opportunity for me to look inward?

I encourage you to mentor and be mentored—and not allow busy-ness to crowd out connection to others.

In his book, *The Mentor Leader*, Tony Dungy, former Super Bowl-winning coach of the Indianapolis Colts, shares a powerful story about resolving to reach out to others even in the face of what appeared to be more urgent and competing priorities.

In 2007, the Colts were set to play the New England Patriots in what many called "The Game of the Century." The Patriots had gone 8–0 and the Colts were 7–0; it was the first time in NFL history that two teams, undefeated after at least seven games, had met up to play.

Mr. Dungy had previously agreed to record a public service announcement [PSA] for The Villages, a foster children's home in the Indianapolis area. The commitment fell on Thursday of the week of the big game and he had a multitude of reasons why he couldn't do it. He argued with himself that the Colts were his employers, not The Villages. He acknowledged the impact the game's outcome would have on his team and their chance to earn a spot in the Super Bowl. He had coaches, players and fans relying on him.

As he reflects on his decision-making process, he recounts, "This truly was a big game…but I'd always told those around me, those same players and coaches, that we needed to find balance in our lives with our priorities. If you start making excuses to cut out the things that are important because of urgent circumstances, it will become a habit, and you'll start cutting them out regularly. You know as well as I do that, whether it's a crisis or not, there always seems to be a reason why *this* time just isn't the *right* time."

Believing it was the right decision for him to make, Coach Dungy left a little early on that Thursday night and took thirty minutes to record the PSA for The Villages. On Sunday, the Colts lost 24–20 on a fourth quarter touchdown by the Patriots, who finished their regular season undefeated and went on to compete in the Super Bowl.

Mr. Dungy shares, "Many people in my position could look back and second-guess that decision to take a half hour away from preparation for the Patriots to help a children's home. If I had watched one more video or gone over one more chart, would we have come up with those four points we needed to win? Would we have ended up in Super Bowl XLII instead of New England? I never lost any sleep over that question, and I will always feel that I gave my best for my team that week."

Two years later, Mr. Dungy continues the story after receiving a post-season letter from a couple in Indiana.

> "[This couple] weren't football fans. They rarely if ever watched Colts games, but they had been watching late-night cable television shortly after the Colts' loss to New England in 'The Game of the Century' two years earlier and had seen a public service announcement—the one I had done for The Villages foster care home. The one I 'didn't really have time to do' but did anyway.

> "Now, the letter informed me, they had a new 12-year-old son in their home—a son who had never been coached in Little League, had never been on a vacation, had never had his own bed. Until now. They went on to tell me what a blessing this boy had become in their lives.

"The letter was a good reminder that we always have time. We always have a platform. There is always someone whose life we can affect—even if we're not aware at the time we're doing it."[7]

Mr. Dungy had a brighter "Yes" burning inside.

Do you?

 Questions to Motivate MentorShift

1. Rate your current "Busy Factor" on a 1–10 scale (10 being the busiest). Do you feel it is in balance? Why or why not?

2. What are some legitimate reasons why you might not feel it's a good time for you to be in a mentoring relationship?

3. What priorities comprise your bigger "Yes?"

CHAPTER 6

Too Boondoggled—
Just Another "Check the Box"

"There's never enough time to do all the nothing you want."
— BILL WATTERSON, CREATOR, "CALVIN AND HOBBES" CARTOON

STORY

boon•dog•gle

> *noun: work of little or no practical value merely to keep or look busy*[8]

I have a friend who frequently drives by a long-standing road construction project. By long-standing, I mean it's been there since just after the Civil War, or so it seems. Whenever he passes it, he starts this comical tirade as he yells at the windshield of his car and cusses out the dashboard,

> "What a *boondoggle!* It's a waste of time and taxpayers' dollars! I'm going to write my congressman, or better yet, go pound on my congressman's door. I'm going to picket in front of the Capitol. I'm offended as a patriotic, true-blue citizen! When is that thing going to be finished?"

I don't think he ever mails a letter, much less darkens the door of any congressional office. I do know that the next time he passes by that intersection, the construction site will still be there and the sight of the orange cones will impel him to deliver the same entertaining outburst.

SUGGESTIONS TO SOLVE THE "TOO BOONDOGGLED" DILEMMA

It's a funny scenario, but it strikes a chord—we all do hate to see or participate in something that we don't perceive has value.

Just as onerous, we dislike participating in something just because it might make us look good for a moment but really holds no meaning for us.

That's the definition of a "boondoggle," and we've all seen them in the workplace. Unfortunately, sometimes a mentoring relationship falls into that category.

When mentoring shows up as a *formal* program, this can easily happen. You might overhear Derek and Travis discussing what you think at first is a conversation about fantasy football picks:

> Derek: "Travis, how many do you need to pick up?"
>
> Travis: "I have two now, how about you?"
>
> Derek: "I have one but I'll pick up another before the end of the year. I signed up for two as part of my annual goals. Do you know any mentees on the market that need to check the box too?"
>
> Travis: "I heard Beau is a free agent. Check with him. His boss is pushing the whole mentoring thing."

Sounds inviting, doesn't it? Not!

In this scenario, the employees are mentoring as an obligatory part of their job. Their yearly rating might suffer if they don't have two mentees to offer up as their prize acquisition.

If mentoring is *informal* in your workplace, you might hear this conversation:

> Erin: "Does it seem like Rico gets lots of management kudos because he mentors Dani?"
>
> Paul: "No kidding. It seems like they think he walks on water."
>
> Erin: "Maybe we need to get on our swim fins and walk on water too."
>
> Paul: "I'll wear swim fins and a striped scuba tank if it helps their perception of me."

I haven't seen many companies that require that you have mentoring as part of your job description, but I do know that it can cause an uptick on your rating if you do. It's an unspoken, non-legislated activity that's viewed favorably even if the company doesn't put much effort into making it happen.

Let's take a step back at this point. Before you ever polish up your annual goals or consider how management might view you for taking part in a mentoring relationship, you need to address the "boondoggle" question first and ask yourself, "Do I think mentoring adds value?"

If the answer is "yes," then your life is easy. Start mentoring or seek out a mentor. You know that it will add worth and develop your skill sets.

If the answer is "no," then this is a thornier issue. If you really don't believe there is anything personally to be gained from mentoring or that the company doesn't stand to benefit from employees helping each other, it's another deal. Then it really is a "check the box" for you at this point.

You might sound like this in a conversation with your colleague:

"Have a mentee?"
"Yup."
"Great, how's it going?"
"It's not bad."
"Awesome. *You can check that box.*"
"I plan to."

Sometimes moving from "boondoggle" into "benefit" simply requires an attitude change.

When it comes to mentoring, your attitudes and motivations will likely fall into one of these three categories:

1. You think mentoring is a waste of time. You do it because you have to.
2. You think mentoring has value. Even then, you do it because you have to.
3. You think mentoring has value. You do it because you want to regardless of your management's position on it.

Here are some response options for you to consider for each category:

1. Either *don't* be in a mentoring relationship (I mean that) or *change* your attitude about it. You want the integrity that comes with acting from your convictions.
2. Get into a mentoring relationship and adjust your attitude. You don't *have* to do anything—you *choose* to.
3. You are already in a positive place and will likely have a constructive mentor or mentee experience.

Rodger Dean Duncan, strategic consultant and author of *Change-Friendly: How to Engage People's Heads, Hearts and Hopes,* refers to a paradigm he calls "The Ladder of Accountability." When it comes to making decisions to change and taking accountability for that change, the rungs look like this:

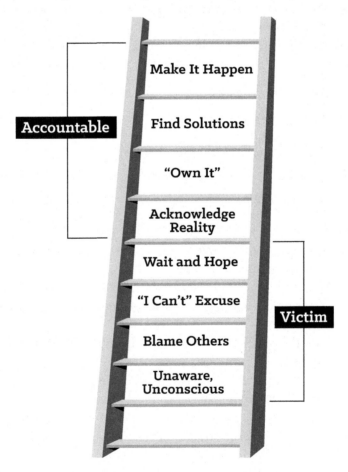

Accountable
- Make It Happen
- Find Solutions
- "Own It"
- Acknowledge Reality

Victim
- Wait and Hope
- "I Can't" Excuse
- Blame Others
- Unaware, Unconscious

In summary, the bottom four rungs represent finger pointing, a "dog ate my homework" outlook, uncontrollable circumstances, and "things happen *to* me." These are victim behaviors.

The top four more productive rungs represent admitting your role in the situation, taking ownership, driving results, and adopting an attitude that "things happen because of me, not to me." These are accountable behaviors.[9]

When it comes to a mentoring relationship, and when you consider your three possible attitudes and responses, where are you on the ladder of accountability?

Will you adjust your perception of mentoring as a "boondoggle" and make change happen *because* of you?

 Questions to Motivate MentorShift

1. How do you feel when you see an activity at work that seems like a "boondoggle?" What's an example?

2. When you consider the Ladder of Accountability, where would you place yourself with regard to mentoring attitudes and behaviors?

3. Where would you like to be on the Ladder? What would you need to do to get there?

CHAPTER 7

Too Binding—
If the Shoe Doesn't Fit, Can I Quit?

"If the shoe doesn't fit, must we change the foot?"
— GLORIA STEINEM, ACTIVIST AND AUTHOR

STORY

Marilyn Monroe once said, "I don't know who invented high heels, but all women owe him a lot."

I could argue that point.

It's true, I loved my navy blue, pointy-toed, 3-inch-high pumps. I also hated them and whoever came up with the whole spiky business.

There is an important fact to know about women. Sometimes if we like a pair of shoes—I mean, *really* like them—we might buy two pairs. Maybe different colors, same style, maybe even the same color, same style.

I mean, when you find a good thing, why not stock up your closet, right?

So my shoe story unfolds, and yes, it is painfully true. It was a typical back-and-forth business trip for me to Washington, D.C. I arrived at my hotel past midnight with plans to be up at the crack of dawn for a 7:00 a.m. meeting downtown. I barely had a chance to hit the mattress, much less contemplate the contents of my baggage.

When I did rummage through my suitcase in the pre-dawn hours, I pulled out my lovely blue shoes—perfect for my chic navy suit of the day. I planned to be dressed to the nines that day for the Washingtonians I would meet. I pulled out both of my pumps.

Both of my *left* navy blue pumps.

41

In my hurry to make my flight the day before, I had grabbed two left shoes from my closet floor.

I had one hour until my meeting and not a shoe store open for hours. I stared sullenly at my shoes in the semi-darkness. My heart sank as I contemplated wearing the flip-flops I'd donned for the airplane trip. No, they wouldn't go with my tailored business suit!

The painful fix was, you guessed it, wear two left shoes. With a jam packed schedule and not a moment to dash into an open shoe store, I walked for seven hours around the streets and offices of downtown Washington in two left shoes.

Two very tight, very tall LEFT shoes.

I cannot share adjectives that described how I felt at 10 that morning… at noon…or at 2 p.m.

If I was near tears over the project proposals I was hearing in my meetings, my clients might have thought they'd presented eye-wateringly bad ideas. But my feet and I knew the truth.

I begged heaven for a chance to sit down and get off my feet.

The meetings lasted till late afternoon but I politely excused myself a couple of hours early that day. As I limped to my cab, I felt justified in my early but timely exit.

Finally granted asylum from the prison of my shoes, I traveled to the airport that evening in my friendly flip-flops. As I settled into my window seat, rubbing my abused right foot and staring at my day planner, I penciled in an appointment with my podiatrist.

SUGGESTIONS TO SOLVE THE "TOO BINDING" DILEMMA

Moral of the story: If the shoe *really* doesn't fit, it's all right to quit!

The link to a mentoring relationship is easy to see, isn't it?

There are things you can do to avoid getting into a Too Binding situation before it occurs and set your relationship up for success. Here are some helpful tips:

- Discuss mentoring objectives at an initial meeting. As you craft your mentoring plan together, commit to certain "check-in points" to make sure the goals are being accomplished. The check-in points are really "How is this going?" talks that can pave the way for some good dialogue with your mentor. (See Appendix A-5 "Creating Expectations" and A-6 "Mid-Course Evaluation" for additional resources.)

- Determine agreed-upon times to check in—at three months, six months? This is flexible and up to you both.
- At these times, commit to discuss a couple of points:
  - Satisfaction points ("I really benefit from attending meetings with you.")
  - Frustration points ("It's tough when we have to keep rescheduling.")

These are important conversations to have *in the beginning* before your mentoring relationship gets into full swing.

Mentee, even after you've taken these proactive steps to ensure success, you may have ended up in a less than satisfying situation. If the relationship is not offering you anything profitable, it's time to re-assess. Mentor, the same is true for you, it goes both ways.

Not all matches are the best fit. A mismatch can occasionally occur if you've been paired with someone through the company matching system or even when you've chosen a mentor yourself. If the chemistry is not there after some earnest effort, it's okay to end the arrangement and go separate ways.

I am not advocating giving up early or being fickle. It's important to work at seeing another's point of view and adjusting to their style. But an exit strategy is essential when the relationship is not what you had both hoped it would be.

Fortunately, most of us don't find ourselves in a "two left shoes" kind of situation. To the contrary, we can usually find a way to fit together and we end up being, at a minimum, the new loafers that take a little breaking in. We just have to wear the relationship for a little while.

And in the most comfortable mentoring relationships, we end up as relaxed and at ease with our mentor or mentee as our favorite scuffed up topsiders or well-worn slippers. The fit is good and we complement one another. We hang on to those shoes for years.

Though my right foot was never the same, yours doesn't have to endure the same drama. If it doesn't fit, you can quit. But better yet, a well-planned choice up front and consistent checking in can assure the best chance of success.

Questions to Motivate MentorShift

1. Have you had a mentoring relationship that you wanted to exit? How did you end it?

2. Why would check-in points be important to you?

3. How would you have an upfront conversation about exit points with your mentor or mentee?

CHAPTER 8

Too Bonding—
Transparency Does Not
Mean Oversharing

"My life is an open book; at least this photo album."
— R. Alan Woods, author

STORY

I once had a mentee I'll call Molly, who within 20 minutes of our first meeting began to overshare. We were still at the initial stages of getting to know one another and I hadn't even gathered all of the basics about her—where she worked, how her job was going, what she wanted out of our mentoring relationship.

Despite this, she immediately began to divulge her feelings about her hateful boss, her tedious marriage, her former gambling addiction and why she thought she should be first in line for a raise. (After all, she'd been nothing but pushed around from Day One.)

Yikes! "How did this happen?" I was thinking to myself.

At that point in time, I was not terribly skilled in culling out what I really was looking for in a mentee and screening them beforehand. Honestly, I had signed up to mentor her without doing an ounce of due diligence. Sigh.

I guess I had this coming: Forewarned would have been forearmed. Even though I considered myself an open and forthright person, I was squirming not only at the topics she felt led to broach and her willingness to proffer up details but also at her direct, out-of-the gate questions to me.

"And what about you, Lori? Can you relate to not getting along with an unreasonable boss? Have you had one like that?"

"And tell me a little bit about you and your family life. Married? Have any kids? I'm eager to get to know all about you and your career."

Well, by that point, I wasn't eager to tell.

"Whoa, let's slow this down a bit." I jumped in and took control of the conversation. "We're going to ratchet this back a bit and start with just some basic information exchange."

I rerouted with, "So, Molly, share with me about when you started with the company and some of the positions you've held."

We did redirect and had a somewhat profitable conversation during that mentoring discussion, but I did not pursue a long-term mentoring relationship with her. I could tell very early on that such an arrangement might have me, like Lucy in the Peanuts cartoon, hanging up my "The Doctor Is In" sign before each meeting.

SUGGESTIONS TO SOLVE THE "TOO BONDING" DILEMMA

Mentor, if you are concerned that you might have to be too forthcoming about yourself and that would feel uncomfortable, here are some ground rules on transparency and self-disclosure for you to consider.

First and most importantly, it's your responsibility to shepherd the level of confidentiality shared.

You can shepherd it in this way: You don't have to share anything about which you don't feel comfortable. Nor do you have to hear the not-so-edifying details of your mentee's personal life. Jump in, stop the conversation, redirect. You are the barometer in terms of how and what type of information is communicated.

We all have a red flag that pops up when someone crosses the line and wants to know too much, too soon.

I can illustrate that in a humorous way. Sometimes when I lead a round-table mentoring group, I like to lighten things up before discussing topics of confidentiality and transparency with this scenario:

I open the meeting and say, "Okay, today we're going to do something different. We are going to go around the circle and everyone is going to share something about themselves that they've never told a living soul. The deeper, darker and juicier, the better. Okay, who wants to go first?"

I keep a serious expression and look expectantly around the table.

I love those three seconds of panic-stricken, "Are you out of your ever-loving mind? Where's the door??" look on their faces. I immediately jump in and say, "Kidding! Did you think I'd really do that to you guys?" (You're making some judgments on the kind of person I really am right now, aren't you?!)

Everyone starts laughing and actually, it really breaks the ice. Then the jokes about the whole prospect of that kind of sharing start to roll.

It was clear in this illustration that I had violated everyone's social norms. Too much, too soon—if ever!

So for you as a mentor, we start with the obvious. Nobody overshares. You drive the appropriateness level. TMI is and always will be just that: Too Much Information.

There are two good guideposts to put in your mentoring relationship up front; a confidentiality agreement and if you feel it's needed, a short list of "open season" and "closed season" topics.

"Open season" might be career goals, job highlights and disappointments, even personnel issues if they can be discussed without violating another person's trust and privacy.

"Closed season" might be damaging information about others, personal family issues, insider information.

Mentee, these guideposts protect you, too. You both will need to navigate those lists for yourselves. I've included a useful tool in the Appendix (A-3 "Confidentiality" and A-5 "Creating Expectations") to help in guiding that conversation.

Let's leave oversharing now and look at normal transparency as a mentor. Recall an element of our initial definition of mentoring that describes it as "mutually sharing your life?" What does that mean, anyway? Simply put, it's allowing your mentee to see honestly and appropriately into your life, both your triumphs and setbacks.

Sometimes even this normal transparency is the real tripping point for mentors.

Mentor, if you are reluctant about being transparent, these might be a few questions you are asking yourself:

- What if my mentee sees me or hears about me in a less than desirable situation?

- What if I don't appear strong and empowered?
- What if I lose control over a situation?
- What if I'm negatively evaluated?

These questions are natural and understandable, yet you can move past them.

Transparency is sharing your accomplishments and setbacks in a healthy, encouraging way and it's not for sissies. It's for those who have an unusual kind of courage. Go at the pace that is comfortable for both of you.

You can do it and it doesn't have to be too bonding.

Now go share something with your mentee or mentor. (And make it juicy.)

 Questions to Motivate MentorShift

1. Have you ever had a mentee or a mentor who has overshared? How did you feel? What did you do?

2. What additional topics might fall under "open" or "closed" season?

3. Why might you feel hesitant about being open and transparent with your mentee? Do you want to change that? If so, how might you do that?

CHAPTER 9

Too Baffling—
Much Experience, None in Mentoring

"Risk comes from not knowing what you're doing."
— WARREN BUFFETT, BILLIONAIRE INVESTOR
AND PHILANTHROPIST

STORY

"Hey, Jamie, Tyler is looking for a mentor. Why don't you mentor him?"

Jamie is a senior sales manager. She is motoring up the company ladder as fast as you can imagine. She has outperformed her sales goals for nine quarters straight. Look up "Most Likely to be V.P. of Sales and Marketing" and you will see her face smiling back at you.

She has talent, results and potential spilling over.

But (keep this to yourself), Jamie has never mentored someone.

Somehow in her 10-year career she has managed to achieve every challenge thrown her way and dazzle her management with brilliance. But when her boss asks her to mentor Tyler, she freezes.

She excuses herself with, "Oh, I'd love to, but our national conference is happening next month, you know, and I'd better focus on that. Maybe after we get that behind us I will have some free time."

The national conference is indeed going to take place next month so she has a plausible out. In reality, she's relieved to be off the hook. She leaves her boss's office thinking, "What would I do with a mentee anyway? I'd feel awkward because I'm not sure exactly what to talk about."

This is more common than you can imagine: Someone who has much experience in the company but none in mentoring.

Whether in a large company with a formal mentoring program or in a small business with informal mentoring, business leaders often don't know what to do in such a role. The more senior and experienced the individual is, the more (privately) embarrassing it can be.

Remember my observation in the book's introduction about sitting at a conference table at prescribed times and dishing out boatloads of advice to a mentee?

I'm convinced this choice occurs by default. Mentor, if you are not sure what is expected of you or don't feel comfortable in that role, you'll default to your comfort zone, which may not be useful at all. For example:

Self: I'm supposed to mentor?

- Since I'm not sure what to do, I'll invite the mentee to come to my office (my office = my comfort zone).
- I'll ask some questions and talk about my career (my career = my comfort zone).
- Then I'll ask about his career (ask questions = no risk)
- Then we'll meet again in a couple of months (delay next meeting = no risk).

SUGGESTIONS TO SOLVE THE "TOO BAFFLING" DILEMMA

If you feel you have "much experience, none in mentoring," there are several effective ways to blast out of your comfort zone and become a mentor, even if for the first time.

Take inventory of your strengths and experience

What do you know how to do very well—right here, right now? Start there. This is an invitation to do an inventory of the experiences, skills and strengths that would absolutely qualify you to be a mentor even if you haven't done it formally before.

What relationships did you have in the past where you taught someone how to do something? What skills and attributes did you use?

Do some strategic risk taking

Learning to mentor is about strategic risk taking. Plan your mentoring opportunities so that you are progressively opening yourself at a comfortable rate. Before you invite your mentee into really difficult situations, you'll want a chance to develop some confidence and build trust with them.

These are possible "high-risk" activities:

- Negotiating the toughest deal you've encountered recently
- Dealing with your most irate client
- Delivering a first-time product to a customer
- Holding a challenging discussion with your boss

These are high-risk examples because the chance of setbacks and self-exposure is considerable. Having a mentor shadowing you at these moments is too much, too soon, perhaps.

You may, however, feel comfortable showing them how to lead an engineering meeting, something you have done very effectively for a long time. You may want to invite your mentee to join you with long-standing clients with whom you've cultivated a profitable, open relationship.

Start with smaller mentoring steps in areas where you feel self-assured and at ease.

Mentor, go through the MentorShift process in Sections 3–6 and plan the steps with your mentee:

- Step 1—You'll identify where you are gifted and experienced and could provide value-added mentoring
- Step 2—You will plan the activities and experiences where your mentee will observe you and contribute to the task at hand
- Step 3—You will plan where and when your mentee will begin to take the lead and how you can reinforce them
- Step 4—You will plan your mentee's "launch" and how you can best support them in the future

You've heard the adage, "An expert in anything was once a beginner." Begin now and soon you will be saying, "Much experience (in my business/company/industry), much in mentoring."

Questions to Motivate MentorShift

1. Have you ever felt like you didn't know exactly what to do in a new mentoring relationship? How did you handle that?

2. Have you done an inventory of your strengths and attributes? In what areas are you comfortable sharing with and teaching others?

3. When you consider inviting a mentee to accompany you at the start of a mentoring relationship, what are "high-risk" and "low-risk" activities for you?

CHAPTER 10

Too Bottomed Out— Stuck to Your Chairs? Mentees Beware!

"To me, if life boils down to one thing, it's movement.
To live is to keep moving."

— JERRY SEINFELD, COMEDIAN

STORY

Do you have a desk job?

My friend, Lisa, does and she playfully related the personal cost of days upon end at her desk, stuck to her chair, with this description:

"Oh my goodness! Midway through the day I would catch a glimpse of my face in a mirror. Perky? No! Pale and pasty? Yes! My skin had an anemic tint from the florescent light that bathes me every moment; my eyes had that glazed look that no amount of mascara would cure and that only my endless hypnotic connection to my computer screen could bring; and the southern hemisphere of my body? Let's just say my posterior region fluctuated between 'numb and numb-er.' I've concluded...I've been imprisoned by my chair!"

What about you? Do you have a love affair with your chair? Do you sit in an office or cubicle all day and when you meet with your mentee, you switch chairs and sit some more?

A recent article in the *L.A. Times*, "Don't Just Sit There. Really." gives us the bottom line on what too many hours on our bottoms can mean.

"Prolonged sitting is not what nature intended for us," says Dr. Camelia Davtyan, clinical professor of medicine at UCLA.

"The chair is out to kill us," says James Levine, an endocrinologist at the Mayo Graduate School of Medicine.

Most of us have years of sitting experience, consider ourselves quite good at it and would swear that nature intended us to do it as much as possible.[10]

Guess what! Real benefits accrue to you when you move out and mentor outside the confines and comforts of your office.

Steven Johnson, author of *Where Good Ideas Come From*, in his widely viewed TED talk[11], shares how moving away from the standard office setting spawns innovation and great ideas. He praises the chaotic scenes of 18th century coffee houses where Enlightenment thought was born, "These type of spaces historically have led to great innovation…places where ideas were likely to come together in new, unpredictable collisions from different backgrounds."

Besides breeding creativity, a move from your chair will better your health.

An *ABC News* piece, "Standing Question: Could Sitting Too Long at Work Be Dangerous?" reported that how long you sit actually changes your body chemistry. Dr. Marc Hamilton discovered that lab mice, when prevented from running around, put on weight. They found that being sedentary turns off an important chemical that burns fat.[12]

I'd prefer to have that fat-burning chemical working full time, wouldn't you?

Here's where the health risks of sitting too long become really scary.

"Sitting is the new smoking," says Anup Kanodia, a physician and researcher at Ohio State University's Wexner Medical Center. As evidence, he cites an Australian study published in October 2012 in the *British Journal of Sports Medicine* that compared the two pastimes. Every hour of TV that people watch, presumably while sitting, cuts about 22 minutes from their life span, the study's authors calculated. By contrast, it's estimated that smokers shorten their lives by about 11 minutes per cigarette."[13]

But wait! Mentor, you like your cubicle or office! You love to sit at your conference table and talk to your mentee. And talk. And sit. And sit some more.

It's nice and comfy there.

What's wrong with this picture?

SUGGESTIONS TO SOLVE THE "TOO BOTTOMED OUT" DILEMMA

The evidence is in! The experts say to stop sitting and start moving to generate more ideas, feel better and increase your life span.

But here's the bottomed out truth: Office life often has your posterior stapled, glued or hammered to your chair. That's just the way it is in offices around the world.

Here's an example: Let's peek through the window of an office building at the Parts Are Parts Company.

On a typical day, if you attached a GPS tracker to the wrist of a manager who is soon to become a mentor, you'd see their trek mapped as they conducted their work. The map would look something like this:

- Arrive at home office
- Home office (2 hours)
- Boss' office (1 hour)
- Conference room (2 hours)
- Cafeteria (10 minutes)
- Colleague's office (1 hour while having lunch)
- Home office (2 hours)
- Home office to parking lot

At the end of this, the map shows car leaving the parking lot. Day is done.

Take note that there are eight hours of sitting at a desk or table and probably 15 minutes of walking from one destination to another. Did that look anything like your typical day?

Do you see some real mentoring challenges here? We are in business and the truth is that some days we aren't like Elvis. We don't even leave the building.

Mentors, here's a question and an action for you. Do you religiously set up your mentoring meetings in your office? Perhaps it's just a habit you aren't even aware that you have?

Here's the action and it's your lead: Take your mentees with you; take them someplace away from the florescent lights and well-worn chairs. The possibilities are limitless and here's where your intentionality and creativity needle must pop to the top of the meter.

There are places to go, things to do, people to see. You can take your mentee with you, including to any...

- Meeting
- Venue
- Conference
- Negotiation
- Outside event
- Business trip
- Coffee shop
- Outdoors (take a walk around your building!)

...where they might benefit from observing and contributing to the real action. Invite them!

Mentor, asking a mentee to join you away from an office setting achieves two goals with one action, a double payoff if you will. You were likely going to any of these places anyway, weren't you? It's an easy way to capitalize on important synergy—your contribution to the event plus a mentee's development at the same time.

Think about everyday opportunities to act intentionally beyond just sitting at your office table for a mentoring conversation. You need to start moving and break the habit of only sitting under the florescent lights for an hour-long meeting.

Stand up to sitting down!

 ## Questions to Motivate MentorShift

1. What are the upsides and downsides of mentoring that involves only conversations in the office?

2. As a mentor, what elements of your job might a mentee find interesting to observe?

3. As a mentee, in what work activities might you like to join your mentor?

CHAPTER 11

Too Blocked—
If At First You
Don't Succeed…Bail?

"If at first you don't succeed, try, try again. Then quit.
There's no point in being a damn fool about it."

— W.C. FIELDS, COMEDIAN AND ACTOR

STORY

W.C. Fields, hush your mouth!

You have to run in the other direction so you don't think like Mr. Fields when it comes to mentoring.

Why? Because "too blocked" is unfortunately "too real," especially when you want to invite a mentee with you.

The other "Too Bs" emanate from attitudes within you. "Too Blocked" comes from external factors, well-meaning or otherwise, that could hinder your success.

Let's think through a few of them so we can prepare you with some work-around solutions.

You are mentoring Lily and you want to take her with you to listen to your customer's comments on your newly submitted proposal. You ask your boss if Lily can accompany you. Here are just a few possible roadblocks. He says:

1. "The audience is meant to be small. We don't need any lookey-loos."
2. "The material is too proprietary. It's only a limited need-to-know audience."

3. "Since you mentioned the idea briefly the other day, I checked with Lily's supervisor. She can't afford to have her away from her job for the whole afternoon."

Here's another possible scenario. Scott, a mechanical engineer, is your mentor. You are both working on the same project and there is a technical meeting out of town to which he has asked you to accompany him. You are in software engineering and there is a natural synergy to be cultivated by your observing the meeting.

You ask your boss for the go-ahead to attend the meeting. Here are a few possible roadblocks. She says,

1. "We don't have the travel budget available."
2. "There's no one to pick up your work while you are gone for a day and a half."
3. "We have that deadline with our client we have to meet, that's more critical."
4. "You haven't persuaded me as to why it's to my benefit for you to go. What will our department gain from it?

These are all legitimate reasons for management to say "no," after all, we are all in business to maximize our profits and satisfy our shareholders. If your management feels that your request is in conflict with company goals, they should decline.

SUGGESTIONS TO SOLVE THE "TOO BLOCKED" DILEMMA

The most important way to pre-emptively work around roadblocks is *to gain your management's buy-in to the mentoring relationship ahead of time.* Both mentor and mentee need management support right from the start. You may still be told "no" from time to time when you request a mentoring opportunity, but you will have engendered a partner in your mission if you have stakeholder backing in advance.

Regarding objections to Lily accompanying you to the meeting, consider these suggestions:

1. A management-mandated small audience is a valid reason that she should not be included. You can explore a couple of options:

- What other customer opportunities might be available?
- Could your boss help you attain permission on a one-time basis from the management a level up?

2. Proprietary material is also a valid reason that she should not attend. You might ask yourself the following:
   - Is there another larger, less proprietary meeting that would reach the same end?
   - If appropriate, could Lily sign a proprietary non-disclosure agreement prior to the meeting so she could attend?
   - Could you attend the meeting and debrief Lily afterwards to the extent that is appropriate?

3. If Lily's boss feels like she can't be absent,
   - Could you and/or your supervisor have a discussion with her supervisor about when she could be away from her assignment?
   - Might you include in that conversation an explanation of the growth opportunities for her and how the mentoring opportunity would benefit both departments?

Regarding objections to the out-of-town meeting with Scott, consider these suggestions:
- No travel budget is a tangible concern and yet such budgets are usually discretionary. It's possible that if you are able to clearly articulate the purpose of the trip and its real benefits, your supervisor might see the usefulness and provide the travel funding. (Your company may have discretion to spend more for travel and less for operating supplies, for example.)* If not, then ask yourself the following:
  - What on-site opportunities might there be for you to observe?
  - Is there a video conferencing capability for this meeting?
  - Is there a webinar capability so that you may watch in real-time or afterwards?

---

* If you are a leader with responsibility for discretionary company finance decisions, please see Appendix A-1, "A Business Case for Mentoring" for further discussion of return on investment for mentoring dollars spent.

Higher education visionary Anthony D'Angelo said, "When solving problems, dig at the roots instead of just hacking at the leaves."[14] That's true when problem solving the roadblocks presented by your management. Dig in and seek to understand the root of *why* they might be preventing the mentoring opportunity so you can more effectively address it.

Be proactive; work any potential impediment up front with your management.

- Make them your partner in achieving mentoring opportunities.
- Communicate its value.
- Show them that you are thinking ahead by offering alternatives to an anticipated "no." Let them know that you understand their reasons.
- Ensure that your own work is done to its highest quality so they don't perceive your mentoring as detracting from what they have hired you to do.

These obstacles are real and, at the same time, can be effectively overcome.

 Questions to Motivate MentorShift

1. Do you have an example of when you wanted to go with your mentor and your boss didn't allow it? How did you handle it?

2. What might be other roadblocks you can think of? How would you address them?

3. Share a time when you were able to convince your management about the benefit of inviting a mentee to go with you.

CHAPTER 12

Resolving to Overcome the Obstacles— Where There's a Will, There's a Way

"If you're trying to achieve, there will be roadblocks. I've had them; everybody has had them. But obstacles don't have to stop you. If you run into a wall, don't turn around and give up. Figure out how to climb it, go through it, or work around it."

— MICHAEL JORDAN, BASKETBALL LEGEND

WHEN IT COMES DOWN TO IT, we always say "yes" when we face "Too Bs or Not Too Bs." Either we say "yes" to commit to our positive inclinations or we say "yes" to agree with our negative deterrents.

It's the proverbial tug-of-war and both sides pull hard. Our decision is the pivotal point in whether good mentoring will happen or not.

As a bright, innovative participant in the workforce, you likely wouldn't be sitting in the seat you occupy were it not for your ability to solve problems and offer creative solutions. So you can either submit to the doubts or you can resolve to work out each one.

Many of these potential solutions offered in the last section, as well as the ones that you might think of, likely will require that you ask something of someone.

This is the first and most important step. Be willing to ask for what you need to become the mentor or mentee that you would like to be. Other solutions may require you to dig deeper into your own self-motivations and expectations.

Key Principle:
If I commit to a mentoring relationship, I must address my hesitations and resolve to solve each.

I have a counselor friend who challenges others by exhorting them, "Go ahead, name your dragons." It's his way of saying that we all need to identify our areas of doubt, reluctance or excuse, name them and look them squarely in their beady little eyes. Then we can slay them.

Be *honest* with yourself as to what holds you back from a mentoring relationship—go ahead, name your dragons! Is it really that you don't have the time? Is it that you feel you don't yet have the knowledge?

You can overcome the obstacles to starting a mentoring relationship. You *can* be a mentor or mentee and a very effective one at that.

In Sections 3–6, The MentorShift Steps, we will walk you through the process, step by step, so that you can win that tug-of-war.

You might even beat a dragon or two.

 Questions to Motivate MentorShift

1. Which of the Seven Too Bs or Not Too Bs could you most relate to?

2. What strategies would you develop in that area so that you can move forward?

3. Are there other Too Bs or Not Too Bs not covered here that might stand in the way of your starting a mentoring relationship?

Prepare for MentorShift— Find and Be the Right Kind of Mentor

"One rose from the right person has more value than a whole garden from the wrong one."

— AUTHOR UNKNOWN

CHAPTER 13

Does a Mentor-in-Shining-Armor Exist?— We Want the Real Deal!

"The real deal is always going to win in the end."
BILL HYBELS, FOUNDER, GLOBAL LEADERSHIP SUMMIT

"ONCE UPON A TIME...as a fair maiden lay weeping upon a cold tombstone, her heartfelt desire was suddenly made real before her: tall, broad of shoulder, attired in gleaming silver and gold, her knight in shining armor had come to rescue his damsel in distress..."[15]

Ahhh, to be rescued and taken away to Happy Forever Land by a Knight in Shining Armor! My pre-adolescent friends and I would talk, giggle and dream about what it would be like when the perfect man came galloping in on the perfect horse at the perfect time to give us the perfect lives!

That hope would burn eternal—or so we planned.

A few years, a few tears and a few bumps in the road later at our twentieth high school reunion we toasted to our lives, and surprisingly, not to our knights in shining armor, but to our real husbands, boyfriends, families, friends and jobs.

Not the perfect, but the real.

Have you ever hoped for something or someone to be absolutely flawless?

How about the perfect mentor? Did you ever sit at your desk and daydream, "If only a high-rolling, upwardly mobile, well-respected giant of industry would swoop in and rescue me from this boring vanilla job that I am living. That would be perfection. My mentor-in-shining-armor would save me from it all!"

Did that mentor show up?

I'm guessing not. And truth be told, you really didn't want that. But you have probably asked yourself, "What qualities would make a really good mentor for me?"

You can Google "What is a Good Mentor" and find, as I did, approximately 71 million results in .27 seconds. That tells me a couple of very enlightening pieces of information.

First, there is an avalanche of data swirling around in the Internet-sphere about what defines a mentor, be it roles, goals, mental credentials or emotional essentials.

Second, supply meets demand. If there are this many mentoring factoids orbiting our Internet universe, it's because there is a demand to know and learn.

People care about mentoring. They want to *find* a mentor. And greater still, they want to *be* a mentor.

Those people are you and me.

So let's answer it. What makes a good mentor?

To answer that, I wouldn't dream of taxing you with an exhaustive list of "Brilliant, Beguiling Mentor Criteria." Besides, I'm guessing you already know the kind of mentor you are looking for or the kind of mentor you want to be. You have probably made your own list.

Instead, I offer up a gold-standard criterion that makes a mentor who rocks. When other mentor criteria fall away, this one characteristic remains.

A good mentor is "the real deal."

My dad used to say admiringly about his own father and lifelong mentor in business, "You know the most impressive thing about Grandpa? He's the genuine article, the real deal."

In my father's jargon, that was a hefty compliment.

Dad meant that Grandpa was a no-fake, transparent man who truthfully shared what he knew. Grandpa's word meant everything to him. Back in the day, he often didn't bother with a business contract—his handshake was his bond. (I know, maybe not a good strategy in today's world!)

More simply put, he was the "what you see is what you get" kind of guy. The real deal.

Some people search for a "mentor-in-shining armor." If they find one, their unrealistic expectations will have the mentor sweating in a rusty metallic suit.

Real mentors can polish up their suits but they also know they have chinks in the metal. They fight a battle and sometimes lose. They admit defeats and they claim marvelous victories.

I don't want someone without any cracks in their armor, do you? I'd like a mentor who, plain and simple, is a genuine person who is real with me.

In the next two chapters, we will eavesdrop on a couple of my conversations with my colleague, Ron. In Chapter 14, you will hear Ron's outcry over the broken state of mentoring in business. He rallies for not only real deal mentors but a shift to a real deal mentoring process as well. In Chapter 15, you'll hear about his connection with Cy, his crusty but compelling former mentor, whose authentic example changed Ron's life.

 Questions to Motivate MentorShift

1. What does "A good mentor is the real deal" mean to you?

2. Describe a mentor who has been genuine and authentic with you. How did they specifically demonstrate these attributes?

3. Are you looking for a mentor-in-shining armor or the real deal? How could overly high expectations of your mentor impact your mentoring relationship?

CHAPTER 14

We Need a Shift— No More Yakking, Tracking, Get Sent Packing

"The best way to escape from a problem is to solve it."

— ALAN SAPORTA, MUSICIAN

"IT'S BROKEN, LORI, flat out broken!" Ron exclaimed. My friend gulped down another bite of his burgeoning Mighty Burger, hurrying to finish so we could continue our discussion.

"We are *missing* a fantastic opportunity to do great mentoring! We miss it because of how we do it...or don't do it. We conduct 'BS-A-Thons!'"

"Ron, that could use a bit more explanation," I countered with amusement.

"You bet," he replied. "Here's current business practice: we construct formal programs where we sit in hour-long obligatory mentoring sessions, stapled to our chairs while yakking at our mentees, then we dismiss the meeting and send them packing with, 'See you next month!'"

Ron's energy spilled over. As we sat at the local burger joint, we'd been engaged in rousing banter about my soon-to-be-released book. He relished adding fuel to my already burning flame about the distressed state of mentoring in business.

Ron feigned a lofty air, looked down at me professorially through his glasses and said, "Or worse, as we talk *at* our mentees, we take on a very important attitude and say, 'Hello, I'm your mentor. What issues can I help *you* deal with today?' The mentor is the dispenser of all wisdom and the mentee is in sleepy 'receive mode.'"

He paused and chuckled at himself. "It feels so contrived at times, just not a process that will drive real change. Then we rack and stack how many mentors and mentees we each have so we can take credit for it in our annual objectives. When we bean count it to death like that, we dilute the heart and soul of what mentoring is all about."

"I understand some of that, Ron," I interjected, "companies want to track metrics so they can judge if they are spending their development dollars effectively."

He continued, "Fair enough. Even then, after we measure it, we 'check the box' and say, 'Yup, our company is a mentoring company, just check our stats.' We feel pretty good about our attempts for a while and we miss the chance to really help people grow! Is that the way it should be?"

"No, it's not, Ron, and that's why I've written the *MentorShift* book."

My ardent friend took a moment to put away a few French fries and then tossed one more volley into our conversation.

"And guess what's happening in the meantime?" Before I could answer, he rejoined, "Employees are walking out the door. And do you know how we address *that*?"

I raised my eyebrows and laughed. "I *do* know, but I bet you will further enlighten me!"

"We hire some outside consultants to come in and fix it!" he crowed.

"Or we just throw in the towel and leave employees to find informal mentoring however and wherever they can," I added.

"Exactly!" Ron cheered me on.

I couldn't help but smile at Ron's impassioned concern about broken mentoring practices because it matched my own. In his heartfelt way, he had illustrated the critical points of why we need a mentor shift.

"Hey Ron, it sounds like you'd agree with me that business mentoring is in need of immediate first aid."

"Absolutely! We need something that feels more real than sitting and looking at each other for an hour under florescent lights."

"Here's a secret, Ron, did you know that companies are sitting on the solution? The answer is right in front of us. I can't wait to share a way to achieve great results with others."

"Sure, let's talk more about the solution…after dessert maybe?"

"Good, I'm up for the Chocolate Brownie Earthquake you suggested earlier."

"And Lori, after the Earthquake, I'll share my near-perfect mentoring experience with you. It's about Cy—he *was* the real deal and he taught me the real way to mentor. I've done my best to follow his lead through the years and not buy in to the yakking, tracking, get sent packing model I just described. He was cool. Be sure to put him in your book."

And that ended Part 1 of my conversation with Ron.

I did put Ron's near-perfect mentoring experience with Cy in the next chapter, because Ron gets it—both why mentoring needs help and what a real deal mentoring relationship can look like.

Till then, what is the mentoring process that Ron protests?

Yakking:
- Mentoring sessions have mentors and mentees stapled, glued and hammered to their chairs under the fluorescent office lights
- Too many one-way conversations where mentor (aka professor!) is dispensing wisdom as the fount of knowledge
- Mentee dutifully listening for the hour-long oration

Tracking:
- Rack up data on mentors and mentees
- Bean count the match-ups to take performance credit for it
- Stack up results to impress the shareholders

Get Sent Packing:
- Mentees are dismissed until next mentoring session
- Employees still walking out the door
- Outside consultants coming in to "fix it"

I protest this process too. How about you?

Maybe it's not quite this broken in your company or maybe it's worse. No wonder Ron longed for the days when he had a real deal mentor who would break that mold and redefine the model.

Let's listen in on Ron and his mentor, Cy.

Questions to Motivate MentorShift

1. Do you think mentoring is broken in your workplace? Why or why not?

2. Can you relate to the "yakking, tracking, get sent packing model"? Describe the scenario you experienced, either as mentor or mentee.

3. Does your company measure the number of mentors and mentees in your organization? Is the metric process helpful? Why or why not?

CHAPTER 15

A Near-Perfect Mentoring Experience— A Real Deal Mentor in Action

"Nothing is perfect. Life is messy. Relationships are complex. Outcomes are uncertain. People are irrational."

— HUGH MACKAY, SOCIAL RESEARCHER AND PROFESSOR

WE'D PUT AWAY THE last decadent bite of the Chocolate Brownie Earthquake when Ron said, "Okay, are you ready to hear my near-perfect mentoring story?"

"Sure, Ron, fire away," I invited, always eager to know the inner workings of a successful mentoring relationship. I was also keenly interested because my instincts told me that the story would have MentorShift principles the whole way through.

Ron began, "I had just moved into a new IT role as a young employee with the company. Doug, a counterpart from another department, invited me to a meeting with Cy, a business director many levels above both of us in the organization.

Doug said, "Come with me to this meeting with Cy because you have IT expertise that will be helpful. But be prepared, he is one rough son of a gun. He will wax you up one side and down the other if he gets a hint that you're not shooting straight with him."

"I prepared like crazy for the meeting. I wasn't going to get caught flat-footed," Ron said.

"We went to the meeting with Cy and apparently he thought I knew my stuff so there was no bloodshed in the meeting.

"Out of the blue, Cy called me a week later. He said, 'I want you to come with me to the quarterly corporate review. You can sit and listen and start getting your feet wet.'

"I was stunned and flattered that he had called me because I didn't report up through his chain and he was an influential guy in the organization. I had no idea what to expect. Over the course of a year that invitation evolved into a seat for me at every quarterly corporate review. After each one, he would put me through an inquisition he called the 'after-action report' with questions like, 'Did you see how the CFO pounced on our cost analysis? He didn't believe it for a minute and he was pressing me to offer up more profit for the quarter.'

"I would have to answer up as to why I thought the CFO had responded as he did and why it was not strategic to reduce the cost estimate at this point. Cy was making me think through it. Then he would tell me why he had answered the CFO's questions as he had and the rationale behind his responses.

"He'd say, 'This is a firm, fixed-price software development job, full of unknown risk and the kind that keeps our corporate leaders and me up at night with worry. It's too early to cut the estimate, Ron. I did that in our last job too soon and paid dearly for my mistake. We have to wait until some more program risk is behind us, then we'll cut the cost estimate.'"

Ron continued, "Trust began building in our relationship and as it did, Cy began to stand me up in front at the corporate reviews to present the IT portion of the review."

"Wasn't that kind of scary, Ron?" I asked. "You were still kind of a young buck at that point."

"I was," he answered, "but Cy was in the audience and he would jump in and help when I needed it." Then Ron rolled his eyes and with a half smile said, "I did stub my toe a couple of times and it was pretty painful. Once I gave out way too much information about what our program cash reserve positions were and as the words were leaving my mouth I saw that look on Cy's face in the audience. I had committed the unpardonable error!"

"Oh, *that* was the scary part," I commiserated.

"Yep, I got taken to the woodshed afterwards—you know that's another way of saying, 'He took a big bite out of my hind quarters!' After the verbal shakedown, he explained why what I had shared was neither financially smart nor politically correct."

"You know it's funny," Ron went on, "he gave me the opportunity to fail. Sure, he did wax me up one side and down the other as Doug had warned. But you know what he did after that?" Ron paused and smiled. "He asked me to give the presentation at the next corporate review."

"He believed in you, Ron." I said. "That's pretty cool."

Ron looked out the window, lost in thought. My ever-effusive friend's demeanor had become reflective.

"You know, Lori, what started out as a tenuous situation with me feeling intimidated by the guy turned into something great. I can't begin to describe everything I learned from him and I emerged a different person than when I went into it. Yes, he was a tough individual but he taught me what being the real deal meant."

"Okay, Ron, this is for the book now. Give me the summary of what made it so good."

Ron laughed. He said, "He gave me an immersive experience, he took me with him to learn the ropes and taught me the personality of the company. He trusted me with not just how to do things but why he did them so I kept working to maintain that trust. He was just an authentic guy."

"I knew your story would be a *MentorShift* story."

He laughed again and picked up the lunch tab. "It's on me, Lori. This has been fun talking about this today."

"Great, Ron…and you paying today? That made it a near-perfect lunch for me!"

Mentors and mentees—here's the good news! The MentorShift system fixes the broken mentoring problem and guides real deal mentors though a real deal process.

Later in this section you will see how you can set up a mentoring relationship from the beginning so that success is just around the corner. You will take a look at these real deal mentors and how to connect with them.

Before we do that, now is a good time for you to pause a moment and take an inventory of your experience in mentoring relationships. Next is Chapter 16, which includes the "What is Mentoring to You?" quiz and the chance to do some reflecting on how mentoring has shown up in your life so far.

 Questions to Motivate MentorShift

1. In your opinion, which elements of Ron's relationship with Cy made it a "near-perfect" mentoring relationship?

2. Why is an immersive experience so important for a mentee?

3. How can a mentor transfer the "unspoken rules" or the personality of the company to a mentee? Why would this be important to do?

CHAPTER 16

What is Mentoring to *YOU*?

Т**AKE THIS QUIZ TO FIND OUT!** Please circle one letter to answer each question.

1. **My frequency as a mentor is as follows:**
   a. None, zippo—period. Ran to take cover in the restroom when the opportunity presented itself.
   b. I have never been a mentor but have had an occasional hankering to be one.
   c. I have been a mentor once.
   d. I have been a mentor many times.

2. **My frequency as a mentee is as follows:**
   a. I am on a superior intellectual and social plane. I can win any friend and influence every person on my own. Mentors—look elsewhere!
   b. I thought about asking someone to mentor me but then opted out at the last minute. I might have missed an opportunity.
   c. I have had a mentor once.
   d. I have had many mentors.

3. **My thoughts about finding a good mentor are as follows:**
   a. One is born every third century and then landing one is like finding the Holy Grail.
   b. I don't know of many although a friend mentioned she knew of a couple good mentors.

    c. You can find a compatible and value-added mentor, but it will probably take some hits and misses.

    d. Good mentors are out there waiting to share the wealth. I will expend some energy to find one.

4. My thoughts about finding a good mentee are as follows:

    a. Aren't mentees either leeches or stalkers!? How would I ever get rid of one once I found them?

    b. I think there are people who could use some mentoring if they were willing to step up.

    c. It's not that difficult to find someone who is willing and committed to be mentored.

    d. Most people have a desire to learn and grow and would welcome some guidance from a trusted mentor.

5. The quality of my experience as a mentor is as follows:

    a. Dire. I think they lined up the Five Most Heinous Mentees of the Year and assigned them to me.

    b. Decent. Our times were fairly comfortable and I would consider doing it again.

    c. Good. My mentees accomplished some of the goals they wanted to work on. I think it was positive overall.

    d. Excellent. I know we both looked forward to the times together and benefited from the relationship.

6. The quality of my experience as a mentee is as follows:

    a. Dreadful. Those mentoring "sessions" were "monologue boot camp" for me. I never knew someone could talk so long without needing to take a breath.

    b. Decent. Our times were fairly comfortable and I would consider doing it again.

    c. Good. My mentor helped me accomplish some of the goals I wanted to accomplish. I think it was positive overall.

    d. Excellent. I know we both looked forward to the times together and benefited from the relationship.

7. **My attitude about mentoring is as follows:**
    a. It's a lame and an unpardonable waste of resources and time but the boss said I have to do it. (Mentor, schmentor.)
    b. Some people benefit, others don't. I think it depends on the match and what they do with their time.
    c. Generally a very good concept.
    d. I'm sold on mentoring and pursue it as part of doing business and in my personal life.

8. **My attitude about developing others as mentors is as follows:**
    a. The only thing I'm developing is a headache. Are we done with this quiz yet?
    b. I think I'm pretty lucky just to develop myself as a mentor. I'm not sure about developing someone else.
    c. It only makes sense to teach others how to mentor so they can do it themselves.
    d. Mentoring will impact the most lives and careers when people teach others how to be a mentor themselves.

How did you do? Go through each of the eight questions and calculate your mentoring score:

A = 1 point
B = 2 points
C = 3 points
D = 4 points

0–8   You aren't a believer—yet! You might have had a less than perfect mentoring relationship in the past or heard an unsuccessful war story or two. But the good news is that you wouldn't be reading this book if somehow you didn't have real interest. You just need some "Triumph Over Doubt" thinking and you'll be on your way. Read on!

9–16   You are open and curious! You've got some questions you want answered and need some more positive experiences. Right now you are reflecting, thinking and analyzing mentoring from all sides. You are close to jumping in with a little more support and encouragement!

17–24   You have dipped your toe in the mentoring waters! You have been willing to be in a mentoring relationship in the past and believe it's a valuable thing to do. You just need a bit more encouragement and instruction. You've taken action already so you are well on your way!

25–32   You are a mentoring guru! Pearls spill forth from your lips and you are a beacon of light to all mentee wanna-bes! You are tuned in to developing others and seek to be mentored yourself. So why read this book if you're already walking on the proverbial mentoring waters? Because I will show you a process to make you BETTER. Good for you and lead the way!

CHAPTER 17

Finding the Right Mentor for You—
A Match Made in Mentoring Heaven?

"He was the toast to her butter."

— NICHOLAS SPARKS, AUTHOR

Wow! "HE WAS the toast to her butter." Now *that's* compatibility. If you're looking for the bright side of matchmaking, that is a compelling metaphor.

On the other hand, you could view the pairing as, "He was the crispy, crusty gluten-filled starch to her greasy, trans-fat emulsified oil."

A good match is in the eye (or maybe the taste buds) of the beholder.

Through the years my single friends have regaled me with hilarious and hopeful stories about their pursuit of a perfect match. I heard the stories of meeting and greeting, make-ups and break-ups, dates that led to disaster and dates that led to mates.

Almost always, the success or failure of the match was dependent upon whether or not it "clicked." What does "click" mean, you ask? It's shorthand for "we had chemistry and there was enough there to take the next step."

Some used online dating services that paired them based on compatibility factors. Ph.D.s had labored over mathematical algorithms that offered the best shot at a winning combination...does a well-calculated poker game come to mind? (I recently read a study stating that 1 in 1,369 dates led to marriage through Match.com's online dating site.[16] That does sound like poker odds, doesn't it?)

Some browsed online profiles and some met for blind dates. Others met through a serendipitous trip to the coffee shop, where they accidentally spilled a sugary beverage on the person next to them and ended up happy in love.

Looking for the right mentor can seem like the same baffling and bewildering pursuit, can't it?

What has your search been like? Have you found a really great mentor with whom you clicked?

Perhaps you've started a mentoring relationship and ended it because there was no chemistry. Maybe you have someone who has enlightened your path for years and to whom you owe thanks until your last breath.

Whether it's love for the ages or a mentoring sage, having the right fit can make or break the experience.

So, the million-dollar question becomes: How do you find a mentor who is suited to you?

There are several pathways, all with varying degrees of success, and they may harken back to the techniques used in matchmaking.

You may find a mentor in one of the following ways:
- Methodical:
  - Your company has a formal matching system fueled with formulas and algorithms that underscore a mathematical formula for mentoring. [Complex software programs + user variables = optimized matches.]
- Matchmaker:
  - Your boss may act as the professional pairer—"Hey, Steve is a good guy. I worked with him on our last software-coding project. Go meet with him and see if he might be a good mentor for you this year."
- Meet-up:
  - Your company holds networking functions whereby you casually or purposely seek someone you might like as a mentor.
- Mentoring Database:
  - Your company has built a list of potential, interested mentors and amassed their information in unique profiles. You can search that database and read their resumes.
- Meaningful Relationship:
  - You already know someone who you believe would be a good mentor. You have a relationship with them already either casually or perhaps you know them well. They have a sound

reputation for helping people and are proficient in what you would like to learn.

There is no one *perfect way* to find a good mentor—*but there are lots of great ways to find a mentor.* All of the methods above I've known to be effective and useful to a seeking mentee.

If you want to be mentored, start doing your research. Look around and listen to peers and co-workers. Talk to your supervisor.

Ask yourself some questions:

- Who has been satisfied with their mentor?
- What made that person a good mentor?
- Who do I respect and admire?
- Who is available to mentor me?

You may hope for someone outside of your department. In a recent article in the *Academy of Management Journal*, it cites that "one of the largest contributing factors for mentee satisfaction is choosing a mentor outside of their respective department."[17] I have seen mentors both within and without a mentee's department work well—so it is your personal preference.

You will want to find someone who has skills and a network that you don't have, someone who is a solid Step 1 – I Do mentor (more on that is coming in Section 3).

After you have identified a person or two who might be a good fit for you, you need to approach them to check their availability and interest.

Let's focus next on how to do the "Big Ask."

 Questions to Motivate MentorShift

1. What are the top three qualities you are seeking in a mentor? Why are they important to you?

2. Have you had a mentoring relationship that did not have a good connection or "click"? What things did you learn from that?

3. Who might you be interested in approaching to mentor you? Think of several potential mentor candidates that might be available for you.

CHAPTER 18

The Big Ask—
If You Don't Ask,
the Answer is Always "No"

"Great things are only possible with outrageous requests."
— THEA ALEXANDER, AUTHOR

A FEW YEARS AGO, I attended the Leadership Investment's "Women's Success Forum" in Denver. I was especially looking forward to a breakout session, "The Fine Art of Small Talk," conducted by Debra Fine, a best-selling speaker and author.

I'd long admired Debra and her humorous advice on artful conversation skills. I intentionally positioned myself in the audience so I'd get an opportunity to speak personally with her. Basically, I sat in the front row of her 200-person workshop and hung on her every word, like a hungry beagle hoping for a treat.

I had just begun my second career as a speaker and writer and needed to sit at the feet of the sages who knew how this business worked.

After the session, I stood by while she spoke with a long line of others while signing her books. I was prepped for the Big Ask and so I sidled up to her when there was a brief break in the action.

"Hi Debra, you don't know me from Adam, but I'm Lori Bachman and I'm just launching a new career as a speaker and writer."

"Hi, Lori." Debra smiled patiently at me.

"I love what you do and I'm looking to do the same kind of thing. That is, speaking and writing on my topic of mentoring. I've spent many years in a large corporation doing mergers and acquisitions and financial planning, so as you can guess, this is a big leap for me."

Debra was still smiling, waiting.

"I can't imagine how busy you must be with all that you do. I'm wondering if you would do me the great favor of having a cup of coffee with me and a chat. I would like to hear about your journey and learn how a successful person like you has traveled this road. I would buy you the best latte you've ever had and you have my word I won't take more than 45 minutes of your time."

I stood there like a little kid in the toy store, wide-eyed and waiting for her response.

Debra studied me for minute, thinking. It seemed like a long minute. Then she smiled and said, "First, Lori, thanks for not asking me for lunch. That's a big time commitment when I'm running my business. You were brave enough to ask me, a total stranger, for coffee though. And you seem so darn earnest, I'll accept your invitation and see if I can help out."

"Thanks, Debra, I really appreciate it. May I have your business card so that I may e-mail you to set it up?"

Debra is generous and warm and so I was fortunate. The Big Ask doesn't always end in a "yes." I've been turned away before. But as a friend of mine says, "If you don't ask, the answer is always 'no.'"

Debra and I did have coffee when her schedule allowed, and in 45 minutes I heard about her instructive and inspiring journey to success.

She has become a mentor to me through her example, by recommending me as a speaker and through conversations on book publishing.

The funny thing now is, Debra and I have become friends. I call her, as well as several others who have graced my path in this way, my "Friend-tor." (Definition: when a mentor morphs into a friend and is someone you just like to hang with, too.)

I told this story to another one of my Friend-tors, Sam Horn, author of *Pop! Create the Perfect Pitch, Title or Tagline for Anything*. She shared this nugget about the Big Ask:

"Once Jack Canfield and I were discussing how we handle a person unknown to us that approaches us and asks for some form of help or mentoring." (Jack Canfield is the co-creator of the *Chicken Soup for the Soul* book series.)

"Jack said that the degree to which he is willing to grant the favor to the asker is directly proportional to the degree to which the asker acknowledges they are asking a favor."

Sam continued, "I agree with Jack, it's important to be humble in requesting the favor of someone's time and to be open about that fact. I have a hunch that is one of the reasons Debra agreed to have an initial meeting with you."

I share this with you because it illustrates a few key points:

- Mentors-in-waiting are out there and willing to help. Keep your eyes open.

- You may be asking a well-known personality, the senior manager down the hall or an executive several levels above you. Always be respectful of their time and commitments when requesting a future conversation. You are asking a favor of them.

- You might not be cold-calling a potential mentor like I did with Debra. You may know the person already. No matter. The same rules of courtesy apply.

- Thank them warmly, whether "yes" or "no." If "yes," keep the ball in your court and take the initiative to make the next meeting arrangements.

A note to mentors: When you get the Big Ask from a mentee-in-waiting, please go easy. You won't necessarily agree to a future commitment, but realize that it takes nerve to summon up courage to ask someone like you for your time and a future conversation.

You were probably in their shoes once, too.

The Big Ask may just be for a one-time cup of coffee and chat or it may be with the hopes of a more enduring relationship.

Recently, Nick, a bright junior engineer, approached me and began to describe his finding-a-mentor dilemma.

"Hey Lori, I want to ask this guy, Pete, to be my mentor. I think he would do it because I know that he has mentored others. He is a great team leader and I want to learn from him."

"Okay, Nick, sounds good so far. How can I help?"

"Well, I don't know how else to say it, but I feel so lame just going up to him and saying 'Dude, you don't know me very well, but will you mentor me?' That just seems so serious and he could entirely blow me off. Isn't there a way to ask it without sounding so…weird? Do I even have to use the word 'mentor?'"

"I agree," I replied. "It could be awkward to approach Pete out of the blue and say that. So how about something like this:

'Hey Pete, I know you're a good team leader and you've helped others before. I have some things I'd like to improve on with my team this year. Would you have some time to talk about what my goals are and some steps I might take? Maybe we would just meet once or maybe more than that. I was just hoping to have a first-time conversation with you.'

"How he responds to this will be a good first signal as to if he's up for helping you further.

"Also, Nick, you've never even said the word mentor as it relates to you and Pete. You are just asking for a slice of his time and counsel. Then when you do meet, that can become your MentorView and you can go from there."

"What's a MentorView, Lori?"

Turn the page and see.

 ## Questions to Motivate MentorShift

1. What is the most difficult thing about approaching someone to ask them to mentor you?

2. If the person says, "No," what would be your response?

3. What will you say and do when the person says, "Yes"?

CHAPTER 19

The MentorView—
Getting to Know You, Getting
to Know More About You

"Death will be a great relief. No more interviews."
— KATHARINE HEPBURN

M s. HEPBURN, were interviews really that bad? I suppose having a long lens paparazzi camera in your face could color your perception of interviews.

But we aren't talking about intrusive interviews, we are talking about the authentic Getting to Know You kind.

We are talking about a MentorView.

What's a MentorView? It's just like it sounds—it's Mentor + Interview = MentorView. It's intentionally making the opportunity to meet and talk with a potential mentor to see if there's common ground to move forward.

You've already established through the Big Ask that the potential mentor is willing to meet with you. So when you've gained access to them, what would ensure the most valuable use of your time together?

Here are a few ideas that could pave the way for a meaningful conversation:

Come prepared with knowledge about your potential mentor
- Where do they shine in terms of sharing expertise?
- What is their background?
- Who else have they mentored?

Take the time to perform some due diligence about them. Skipping that can lead to a less-than-positive connection.

Once I interviewed in-house for a lateral job position. I felt like it was a slam-dunk that I would get the cross-training opportunity. I had worked in the area previously and knew the players. It was all wrapped up.

Or so I thought. I went into the interview and casually chatted up my potential new boss. I asked a few questions. I thanked him for his time and left feeling that the job was mine.

When do I move in my stuff?

About two weeks later, my current boss, Clark, called to give me feedback on the interview. He shared, "Lori, you came across as unprepared, like you had not taken the time to see what was currently happening in the product area. I know you worked there in the past but you can't rely on only that."

The product area continued to interview other candidates.

I learned to study up and come in prepared. It was a bit embarrassing that I had neglected to do something as simple as knowing the available data on the projects and personnel.

That won't happen again! So although my experience was job-related, I encourage you to go into the MentorView having done your exploratory homework. Here is a list of information sources on your potential mentor's (or mentee's) background:

- LinkedIN—essentially a snapshot of a resume
- Any company Interweb tools you may have
- Google search for their personal sites/blogs
- Google Scholar to see if they have been published or mentioned in any academic research
- If you were connected by a friend/acquaintance/HR department, ask them for background information before the first meeting

Be ready to articulate what you are looking for in terms of their potential investment in you, should you decide to move forward

- Do you hope for consistently scheduled meetings?
- Do you want a drop-by arrangement when you encounter certain challenges on an as-needed basis?
- What topics or areas of interest will you want to discuss?
- What goals are you working to achieve?

- How can they help with that?
- What timeframe are you hoping for? Weeks? Months?

Mentors appreciate a potential mentee who knows what they are looking for and can express it. It helps make the decision to engage in a mentoring relationship more straightforward.

Gauge the chemistry (click) with the potential mentor

There's that matchmaking thing again! There's something to be said for a relaxed give-and-take conversation where you have the feeling, "I can relate to this person."

The difference between a job interview and a MentorView is that some job interviews are mandatory. You *need* the job and it will provide your immediate bread and butter.

A MentorView is much more enjoyable and comfortable. You *want* a mentor but your paycheck probably won't stop tomorrow if you don't have one today.

You are there because you want to grow and develop professionally and personally. Your mentor may even grow into a Friend-tor and move beyond your work life. So prepare well and enjoy the process.

Next, we will meet the MentorViewers.

 Questions to Motivate MentorShift

1. Does the thought of a MentorView seem fun or nerve-racking? Why?

2. In my bumbled job interview story, what attitudes or actions did I exhibit that made my interviewer say, "Next, please"? How might you improve on that?

3. What questions are important to ask a potential mentor? (For a list of additional insightful questions to ask a potential mentor (or mentee) during a MentorView, see Appendix A-2 "More Questions for the MentorView.")

CHAPTER 20

Meet the MentorViewers— Engaging with the "ForMentors"

"I love the early process of asking questions about a story and deciding which questions matter most."

— DIANE SAWYER, NEWS ANCHOR

A S WE CONCLUDE THIS SECTION on finding and becoming the right kind of mentor, we meet Jeb and Sami, our two central characters, who are both mentors in the making and dedicated to finding a good mentor fit. As we just discussed, they are:

- Prepared with knowledge about the potential mentor
- Ready to articulate what they are looking for in terms of the mentor's investment in them
- Wanting to gauge the chemistry (click) with the potential mentor

In the next four chapters, they introduce themselves to four "ForMentors" who, like all of us, have a few lively personality traits here and there, but who begin to shape Jeb and Sami's picture of what good mentoring is all about.

Why are they called "ForMentors?" Because they are keenly and enthusiastically *for* the growth and development of their potential mentee. These are a few examples of real-deal mentors to seek out and emulate.

Each chapter:

- Portrays a comfortable and informal way to approach the MentorView

- Offers you insight into four real-deal mentor attributes exemplified by each ForMentor.*
  - ○ Goal-setting mindset (The "AchieveMentor")
  - ○ Productive, relaxed approach to relationships (The "EnjoyMentor")
  - ○ Personal presence and self-assurance (The "DevelopMentor")
  - ○ Constancy and dependability (The "CommitMentor")

Each chapter begins with the MentorView, then asks the question, "Could you benefit from this mentor?" and offers specific tips for incorporating that mentor characteristic into your life.

Mentees, you will certainly recognize some mentors you've known in the portrayals that follow. And mentors, be sure to ask yourselves, "Do I model these qualities for my mentees?"

As you watch Jeb and Sami ask questions and conduct their MentorViews, you're sure to learn more about finding and being the right kind of mentor.

Then, it's on to the Four Steps.

---

* At a later point, you may wish to check out Appendix A-7, "The TorMentors"

CHAPTER 21

MentorView #1

The AchieveMentor— He Rolls with Your Goals and Sets You Up To Score

If you're bored with life—you don't get up every morning with a burning desire to do things—you don't have enough goals.

— LOU HOLTZ, RETIRED FOOTBALL COACH,
COLLEGE FOOTBALL HALL OF FAME

a•chieve•mentor

1. A mentor who understands the importance of setting and reaching goals
2. A mentor who is well versed in long- and short-term goal setting methods and encourages mentee to jump in
3. Mentee might be found tossing an occasional 2-pointer into the office plastic b-ball hoop; after all, goals are goals, aren't they?

MentorView:

Sami enters Adam's office and looks around, wide-eyed and amused, at the sports paraphernalia adorning his walls.

"Am I at the right place, 'Adam's Sporting Goods?'"

Adam looks up from his desk and laughs. "You've got it, Sami, I could open up shop. Maybe a tad overdone, but my office is my castle...or as my wife would say, my stadium. Isn't it great?"

Sami does not respond.

"You don't have to answer that! Hey, I'm so glad you made it over to talk with me about your goals. You mentioned that you're trying to plan out what you might like to do with your career long-term?"

"Yes," Sami replies. "I want to make a career development plan and I don't really know how to get started. Would you have some time to work with me on it?"

"I'll make the time. I know that it is kind of hard for anyone to envision what they want to do in five or 10 years. But if you don't do that, it will be like the saying goes, 'If you don't know where you're going, you'll end up someplace else.' Hey, by the way, do you know who said that?"

Sami smiles. "Yogi Berra, who incidentally played for the New York Yankees most of his career. Arguably the best catcher ever to play the game and inducted into the Baseball Hall of Fame in 1972. Who doesn't know that?"

Adam laughs heartily. "Score! This goal-setting exercise is going to be great! Okay, let's get started. Have you heard of SMART goal setting? SMART stands for Specific, Measurable, Achievable, Relevant and Time-Bound. Sounds like a mouthful but it's a pretty good way to start looking at what you want to accomplish both in the short and long run.

"First, Sami, let's take a look at the job assignments that you've really enjoyed and what specifically you liked about each of them."

"Great," Sami replies. "I started out in software design as my first position here. I liked developing requirements for applications but wasn't crazy about actually programming code…"

(An hour later)

"Okay, thanks, Adam, this has been really helpful. I'll go work on these ideas and put some specific objectives and timeframes on them."

"Good, want to get back together next week, Sami?"

"Let's make it two weeks. I want to put some brainpower into these and make sure I do it right."

Sami turns to leave Adam's office. As she walks out the door she adds, "Speaking of that, do you know who said, 'If you don't have time to do it right, when will you have time to do it over?'"

Adam raises his eyebrows, laughs and replies, "John Wooden…who doesn't know that?!"

Could you benefit from an AchieveMentor in your life?

Business author Brian Tracy says, "People with clear, written goals, accomplish far more in a shorter period of time than people without them could ever imagine."[18]

How about you? Do you have clear, measurable goals?

Here are two ways a mentor can help with that. Let's go back to the AchieveMentor's SMART goals. Ask your mentor to work with you on some goals that follow those guidelines—Specific, Measurable, Achievable, Relevant and Time-Bound. Most of the time people (if they manage to write their goals down at all) come up with not-so-smart goals. Let's compare:

Not-so-SMART

Not-so-specific	"I want to be a better trainer."
Not-so-measurable	"I want to mentor lots of mentees."
Not-so-achievable	"I will earn an MBA in three months."
Not-so-relevant	"I will train my employees in basket weaving."
Not-so-time-bound	"I will start a mastermind group."

SMART

Specific	"I will train three groups next month."
Measurable	"I will mentor two mentees by year end."
Achievable	"I will earn an MBA in two years."
Relevant	"I will train my employees in giving feedback."
Time-bound	"I will start a mastermind group in first quarter."

Make your goals SMART so that you will know when you have achieved them. You get the idea.

A second way an AchieveMentor can help to set goals is more short-term—in fact it takes 30 days. I urge you to take the time to watch Matt Cutts, Google engineer, as he delivers a three-minute TED (Technology, Entertainment and Design) talk entitled "Try Something New for Thirty Days."[19]

Matt begins his talk, "A few years ago, I felt like I was stuck in a rut, so I decided to follow in the footsteps of the great American philosopher, Morgan Spurlock, and try something new for 30 days.

"Morgan Spurlock created the documentary film, *Super Size Me*, which depicts an experiment he conducted in 2003, in which he ate nothing but three McDonald's fast food meals a day every day for 30 days. The result wasn't pretty!"

Matt continues, "The idea is actually pretty simple. Think about something you've always wanted to add to your life and try it for the next 30 days. It turns out that 30 days is just about the right amount of time to add a new habit or subtract a habit, like watching the news, from your life."

Matt describes the ventures he added to and subtracted from his life for 30 days at a time—he took a photo every day, worked on a novel, biked to work, gave up sugar, TV and Twitter—each for 30 days.

Matt's payoff, "…instead of the months flying by, forgotten, the time became much more memorable…and my self-confidence grew."

Mentor, you and your mentee can brainstorm on those short-term ideas (some may even be work-related!) that are small steps but create a big personal ROI over the long term. You can help your mentee start with small steps that follow the SMART guidelines.

Mentee, work with your AchieveMentor to create and achieve your goals. After all, as a famous person once said, "What keeps me going is goals."

Do you know who said that?*

 Questions to Motivate MentorShift

1. In the past, have you created goals for yourself? What are a few—at work and outside of work?

2. Think of a goal you would like to accomplish now. Write it down as a SMART goal.

3. Why do you think it is important to write down your goals and talk about them with a mentor?

---

*   Muhammad Ali!

CHAPTER 22

MentorView #2
The EnjoyMentor—
Chai or Chardonnay?
She'll Chill With You Any Day

"Just play. Have fun. Enjoy the game."
— MICHAEL JORDAN

en•joy•men•tor

1. Also referred to as a Drop-in-Mentor: Invites her mentee to pop into the cubicle and set up an impromptu meeting or grab a bit of advice
2. Mentor was a wine sommelier, bartender, coffee shop barista and professional tea taster in a former life. There is no beverage upon which she cannot make a recommendation
3. Mentee can be found in relaxed conversation with her mentor as they enjoy an informal catch-up meeting outside of the office

The MentorView:

Sami peeks inside Emma's cubicle. Emma is sitting up straight on a large blue exercise ball as she types at her keyboard, earbuds in her ears.

"Excuse me, Emma, could I grab a quick minute of your time?"

Emma looks up from her desk, pulling off the earphones, "Oh hey, Sami, come in. I remember that we met at the project meeting last week. How are things in your world?"

99

Sami surveys Emma's surroundings. Her cubicle looks like a busy, colorful Pinterest site, loaded with her personality and interests. Two photos of her golden retriever, a photo of herself and her boyfriend on a hike, a couple of team awards and a sign that says, "Nobody *REALLY* knows what is going on around here."

"Things are good." Sami replies. "I wondered if you'd be open to meet for an hour to talk about a job opportunity I have. If so, would you mind if we met off site, maybe Perky Jerk's Coffee down the street? Since it's about a job change, I didn't want to draw too much attention here at work. So it's kind of a stealth meeting."

"Excellent!" Emma laughs, "My favorite kind! We can get all the world's top secret problems solved!" She studies her calendar and says, "I'm happy to meet, how about Thursday at 5:30?"

"Nice, let's plan on it. Thanks, Emma."

(One month later)

"So Emma, you probably heard I got the job, now I'm trying to figure out my new boss. She's a different character, that's for sure. Actually, she's a real piece of work! I just need to run some stuff by you."

"Sure, I used to work in that area so I kind of know what's up. Let's do same place, same time, this Tuesday after work?"

(Six months later via Skype)

"Hey Emma, how's life?"

"Not bad, Sami, how's the new job going? Are you adjusting to life in San Diego? That's a tough assignment but somebody's got to do it. Get any surfing in yet?"

"Ha, not really! I've been stuck in here for 10-hour days the past three weeks. I'm ready for a break. Are you coming out this way anytime soon?"

"Next month I will be there. Grab dinner at Hasta La Bye Bye's? I've been missing the best Mexican food on the planet and the margaritas are calling my name."

"Great. Let's be sure to talk about both of our projects in between the 'Endless Basket of Chips,' okay?"

"Sounds good to me. I'll be in touch."

❋   ❋   ❋

Could you benefit from an EnjoyMentor?

Although many mentoring relationships might be more committed and meet more frequently, EnjoyMentors are there when you need them.

You may not meet for long stretches of time. You may discuss one topic this time and a totally different topic the next.

You might never really meet in an office setting because you both enjoy a more relaxed place. This mentor can easily morph into the Friend-tor described earlier and may often just want to meet on a social basis.

Before we leave the EnjoyMentor, it's worthwhile to ask, "Are there any potential pitfalls to an EnjoyMentor?"

This is one ForMentor that requires an additional dose of maturity and discretion about boundaries. All of us are over 21 and know the possible pitfalls of a male/female mentoring pair spending too much time outside of the office in a social setting, particularly without spouses present. So use good judgment!

Okay, with all that in place, make good choices and enjoy your EnjoyMentor. If an EnjoyMentor becomes totally, 100% a friend and that works for both parties, great!

Sometimes you just need a mentor whom you can call with a question, or ask for some feedback.

When I think of John C. Crosby's quote, "Mentoring is a brain to pick, an ear to listen and a push in the right direction,"[21] I think of the EnjoyMentor.

 Questions to Motivate MentorShift

1. Do you have an EnjoyMentor? What is that relationship like and how did it get started?

2. What are the benefits of time spent with your mentor in a more relaxed setting?

3. Have you tried the 2007 Jordan Cabernet? A seamless wine, that exudes beautiful, dense blackberry aromas that echo through the mid-palate. My EnjoyMentor recommended it.

CHAPTER 23

MentorView #3
The DevelopMentor—
With a Little Spit and Polish, He'll Get
You Groomed for Greatness

"Cuz every girl's crazy 'bout a sharp-dressed man."

— ZZ TOP, ROCK BAND

de•vel•op•mentor

1. A mentor who will often be seen articulately conversing with colleagues and higher ups, dressed for success and brandishing a charming smile (sincere, of course)
2. A mentor who knows the what and wherefores of social grace and charm. He is able to command a presence as he enters a room. Men, women, children and household pets stand at attention when he is around
3. His mentee can be found perusing Forbes, Harvard Business Review…and an occasional issue of GQ

The MentorView:

"Hey Dan, thanks for taking some time to meet with me," Jeb opens.

"No worries, I'm glad to help out if I can. What's up?"

"Well, I have some opportunities to go to some really big meetings back East. Probably a couple in Europe this spring, too. Our project content is really tight; we feel good about our offerings. In fact, we've aced our competitors on this type of deal the last two times we ran up against them."

"Sounds good, Jeb, it seems like it's in the bag. I'm not really clear on how I can help?"

"Well, at the risk of sounding superficial and desperate, I need some help with my presence. That includes some tips on how to meet these guys, impress them right off the bat. And I suppose I shouldn't dress like an idiot either. And uh…you don't have to mention that I'm asking about this to anyone. I think I should know this presence stuff already."

Dan grins and replies, "No problem, man, I'm willing to give you my ideas for what they're worth. It's funny you're asking me about this. The company actually sent me to something called 'Executive Finishing School for Tomorrow's Leaders' several years back. We all secretly called it charm school. They must have thought I was the poster boy for most in need of manners or something! All I know is that I needed some help.

"They even hired a coach for me since I was going to be meeting regularly with the big dogs across industry. I guess they figured I was representing the company so they needed to invest in me."

"What did charm school and your coach help you with?"

"A ton of things—introductions, business attire, corporate gift etiquette, dealing with ethnic differences. The list goes on. They were standing me up straight and tall, showing me how to greet someone from another country—and practically wiping off my mouth if a crumb dropped at dinner. It was intense!"

Jeb laughs. "It sounds intense. If you were a poster boy, then I'd be hanging right up there with you! Would you be up for meeting a few times with me to go through some of that stuff?"

"Sure, we can make some time to do that. Let's shoot for next week and we can start going through some of what they taught me. Hey, and next time you come by, Jeb, try tucking in your shirt and getting the coffee stain off your sleeve first. Then I'll know there's hope for you."

Jeb laughs and shakes his head as he turns to leave. "Thanks and see you next week. I'll be sure to wear my tux and tails."

❋   ❋   ❋

Could you benefit from a DevelopMentor?

No matter what our upbringing has been or whose personal style and presence we admire, we could all use some mentoring help on looking and acting the part.

I used to have a boss we had nicknamed "Gucci" who knew how to do just that. He came by the nickname honestly because he had a sense of fashion and panache unbeknownst to the rest of us regular slovenly souls.

He was quite proper and had served in the British Royal Navy. For years, he came to work dressed in Savile Row suits, Hermes ties, Brooks Brothers cuff links, a Cartier watch and of course, sleek Gucci shoes.

When the rest of the guys in the office wore a sports coat, he wore a suit. When they came in for a Saturday meeting dressed in jeans and T-Shirts, he wore pressed khakis and a Polo shirt. His world was turned upside down when the company went to business casual five days a week. He spoke of his closeted Hermes ties at home as if they were long lost friends.

Not only did he dress to the nines, he possessed a certain swagger that others experienced as supreme confidence. He was not a tall man but would remind those around him, "Stand to the full height of your stature."

He would say, "Look sharp, act sharp, be sharp. Word travels."

To this day, whenever people quote something he said, they imitate his British accent and the way he stood and delivered. He had the presence and knew the protocols.

We all know that there is more to developing another person than just the external persona and pedigree but it is often a part that is overlooked.

It shouldn't be.

Remember hearing, "You'll never get a second chance to make a first impression?" Researchers from NYU found that we make 11 major decisions about one another in the first seven seconds of meeting.[22] First impressions are swiftly made and can become lasting ones.

As for lasting impressions, what is your presence as you come to the office each day?

How many executives and employees have you seen who come to work looking like an unmade bed? (Remember the days of combing one's hair before leaving the house? Hair gel can't solve every grooming gaffe!)

And what about ar-tick-u-lay-shun? I know one company president who said "um" about every third word and mumbled when he gave a presentation. Weren't our fearless leaders supposed to be eloquent and command our attention?

An honest and tactful mentor can often help you with these elements of presence, protocol and appearance.

When you are with your mentor, you can watch and learn practical and necessary business practices such as how to:

- Introduce yourself effectively
- Articulate your company and project brand
- Portray confident body language
- Choose appropriate dress for formal, business or business casual settings
- Mind your manners at company functions
- Navigate unspoken business etiquette such as picking up the check, giving corporate gifts, communicating in the boardroom

Look for at least one person who can be a DevelopMentor for you. It's good to look sharp, act sharp, be sharp.

Oh, one last thing I couldn't help but noticing—is that a spot of mustard on your tie?

 ## Questions to Motivate MentorShift

1. Who is a mentor you've known who lived the motto, "look sharp, act sharp, be sharp"?

2. How does someone's "personal presence" impact you?

3. Rate yourself on "personal presence" on a 1–10 scale. In what areas specifically could a mentor help you? Who might that mentor be?

CHAPTER 24

MentorView #4

The CommitMentor— She'll Be With You To Infinity and Beyond

"Unless commitment is made there are only promises and hopes…but no plans."

— PETER DRUCKER, MANAGEMENT EXPERT

com•mit•mentor

1. A mentor committed to their mentee's growth over the short haul
2. A mentor committed to their mentee's growth over the long haul
3. Mentee can be found conquering heights they never knew possible

Jeb looks around the coffee shop. Callie has asked him to meet up with her and some friends after work. As he scans the clusters of people gathered, his gaze stops at a group in the far corner, laughing, with one of the guys standing up and making sweeping gestures with his arms as if playing charades. Jeb spies Callie in the midst of the group, laughing and pointing at the man standing.

Callie spots Jeb and enthusiastically motions him over. "Jeb, come join us. Sam was just entertaining us with his story of how he spoke to an audience of 500 people. He's showing us his newly acquired skill, 'Large audiences, large gestures.' Doesn't he look like a loon doing that here in a coffee shop?"

Sam interrupts, "A loon? How dare you speak to the someday recipient of the elite Distinguished Toastmaster's Award!?"

Chris cuts in, "You might be the next Distinguished Toastmaster, Sam, but I think this establishment is going to ask you to leave. You're driving away business and frightening children. You better go order a half dozen coffees to stay in their good graces."

Everyone laughs as Sam shrugs, bows and takes his seat.

"Guys, can you take a minute and show some manners?" Callie interjects. "Meet Jeb. He didn't know what he was getting into but I invited him because we talked about doing some mentoring over the next few months."

"Jeb, you're going to let Callie mentor you and drag you into this questionable company?" Sam laughs.

"Hi, everyone. Actually, Callie did *not* mention what I was getting myself into. She just said come hang out with some of her friends."

"Well, we will all gladly admit that Callie is our friend. In fact, we call her our "Friend-tor" because she actually had a hand in mentoring each one of us in some way or another," says Tiffany.

"Although it's been a while since we fell regularly under her most excellent tutelage," Chris chimes in. "Good thing we meet up here occasionally so she can keep us tuned up."

"A tough job!" Callie replies. "Yes, Jeb, I have had a mentoring role with each of these three, all in different capacities. None of it was or is formal and they've all actually moved on to new horizons. But we still meet a few times a year to make sure everyone is doing okay."

"It's actually pretty helpful because we stay connected with her and with each other—like getting up to speed on Sam's new speaking career," Tiffany offers.

Callie smiles and says, "Jeb, you are certainly welcome to join our group. It's a great connection that we keep and we've been staying in touch for a couple of years."

"Outstanding!" Tiffany chimes in. "We welcome newcomers to our group. Jeb, did you know that the new guy *always* picks up the tab?"

※   ※   ※

Could you benefit from a CommitMentor?
A CommitMentor invests in their mentee, whether it's for a short time, long term, or maybe even "to infinity and beyond!"

What are the marks of a CommitMentor?

My mountaineering guide and friend, J.T., offered a noteworthy example and a proven process that a mentor can follow in the workplace and beyond.

Marks of a CommitMentor

J.T. taught me how to climb mountains. In Colorado, you can earn your badge of courage by engaging in all that the great outdoors has to offer. One of those ways is by trekking up, scrambling over and hanging on for dear life to any of its 50-odd 14,000-foot peaks. J.T. determined, with my enthusiastic agreement, that we would conquer some of those mountains, literally.

As a CommitMentor he was truly a "share by showing" guy and he led me up the path to success in several ways.

Preparation

J.T. was always suited up in the latest recreational gear. "Hey, check out my new high altitude watch—it's calibrated to measure how high we are to the meter." He ensured that I had all the right trappings and supplies. "Do you have all of your energy bars? Here, try these, they are loaded with protein and carbs."

Practice

He started me out on so-called easy peaks (according to whose standards, I asked?). We took day hikes to local areas with only 2,000 feet of vertical gain, up to a 7,000-foot top elevation. "Your legs and lungs need to learn what it feels like," J.T. would counsel. I got my first taste of what it would feel like to summit from those easy peaks.

Perseverance

Mountain climbing can be risky business. On one of our hikes, our guide took us through a route that was, frankly, far above my skill level.

To make matters worse, an early afternoon snowstorm blew in within a matter of minutes. I couldn't see in front of me as I clung motionlessly to a rock.

J.T. made it a practice to climb behind me so that he could catch whatever I dropped and could shout up encouragement and advice: "Grab on to that handhold on your right, up about a foot." We hung on until the storm subsided and J.T. basically talked me up the mountain that day. Over and over he coached, "You can do it, Lori. I'm right here behind you. You can do it."

Party and Praise

J.T. was right—I did it! As we summited that day, he grinned at me and said, "Piece of cake. You were awesome today and I had your back all the way." And he had.

Exhausted and exhilarated, I gazed out as I sat perched on a rock at the summit, enjoying my peanut butter sandwich and beef jerky (and fifth energy bar). I reflected on the past months as J.T. had pressed on me to prepare and practice. I was glad to have a CommitMentor.

One mark of a CommitMentor is that you still carry their words and actions with you after you see them no more. J.T. is climbing heavenly mountains now, but I will always remember his commitment to my welfare and accomplishment. I smile as I hear his words in my head, "Have another energy bar, you'll need it for this next stretch."

Rick Warren, best-selling author of *The Purpose Driven Life,* said, "Nothing shapes your life more than the commitments you choose to make."[24]

How about you—will you be a CommitMentor?

 Questions to Motivate MentorShift

1. Does mentoring have to be for the long term to be committed? Why or why not?

2. Which of the marks of a CommitMentor could you most relate to?

3. Have you had a CommitMentor? Describe their qualities and their impact on you.

Did you meet any ForMentors who particularly impressed you with their good mentoring attributes?

Throughout Part 1, I hope you've done some productive thinking about how to resolve your mentor tension and how to find and be the right kind of mentor. *This has been essential groundwork.*

Now that you are prepared to continue on with your mentoring relationship, Part 2 "Mobilize the Steps, Multiply the Future," guides you through the practice of the MentorShift Four Steps.

Section 3, KNOW. (Step 1 – I Do) shines the spotlight first on mentors. We'll examine your strengths and what you have to offer a mentee to get the process rolling.

PART 2

Mobilize The Steps, Multiply the Future

"Faith is taking the first step even when you don't see the whole staircase."
— MARTIN LUTHER KING, JR.

CHAPTER 25

The Four-Step MentorShift Process—KNOW. SHOW. GROW. GO.

"Nobody cares if you can't dance well. Just get up and dance."
— DAVE BARRY, HUMORIST

I DON'T CARE HOW YOUNG OR OLD, buffed up or broken down you are—you've tried to dance "Gangnam Style" at least once, right?

Even if it's in the privacy of your own living room with the curtains closed and doors dead-bolted, you cranked up the volume, hopped around as you watched the rapper Psy ride the imaginary horse and laughed at yourself when you totally bungled the steps.

Come on, admit it, your secret is safe here.

We like to learn steps we can remember and relate to, don't we? They give us a feeling of accomplishment, whether someone sees us or not.

Whenever, however, wherever you have danced in your life—that's the way you learned.

We absorb a lot of life like that. Psychologists tell us that categorization is the basic motive of our minds. We all have a deep need to categorize (name/group/file) everything we encounter in life. When we categorize effectively, our brains learn.[25]

Consider these—

- Ten Steps to Achieving Financial Success
- Eight Healthy Hints to a New You
- Five Steps to Buying a New Car
- Fifty Ways to Leave Your Lover

When a process or system is categorized into steps, we can grab onto it.

In 1965, professor and author Bruce Tuckman created his team-development model that explains how teams come together and solidify. He devised these steps:

- Forming (eager team members, leader-dependent)
- Storming (clashes for control)
- Norming (agreement and consensus form)
- Performing (shared vision, group autonomy)

Catchy, yes? Recently I participated in a new venture that was in the midst of some chaotic beginnings. In a meeting, the team leader said, "Everyone, realize where we are in the process. We are in the storming phase. It's going to get better in the norming stage."

Forty years after its creation, Tuckman's four steps still effectively described the process in a way the team could understand.

MentorShift is about steps. Four steps that you learn to do with someone; four steps that you can relate to and remember.

Here' s a top-level view:

Step 1 – KNOW. (I Do)

Mentors must *know* their subject matter well as they share knowledge; they *know* the skills and talents they confidently possess to best benefit their mentees

Step 2 – SHOW. (I Do, You Contribute)

Mentors *show* their mentees the skill/talent/task as the mentee observes; Mentee contributes to the task to strengthen learning

Step 3 – GROW. (You Do, I Contribute)

Mentees *grow* as they move forward into the leadership role; Mentor contributes by offering encouragement and support

Step 4 – GO. (You Do)

Mentees have become fully independent and equipped to *go* perform the task; Mentors *go* on to mentor again

These stages aren't cemented in concrete with a precise end to one step and a definitive start to the next. Like most systems, you will start, stop and reconfigure. You may go back a step for a while. But you will end up ultimately moving from KNOW to GO.

Remember Judson Laippley? He's the comic who rose to meteoric YouTube stardom when he performed his "Evolution of Dance." It's hilarious and worth noting this—*with his steps we all can relate to and remember*, it's no wonder it received over 200 million YouTube views.

MentorShift is like that. It contains steps we all can relate to and remember. (Minus the post to YouTube.) In Sections 3–6 you will walk through each of the MentorShift steps in detail. As you go through them, you will see:

- What each step holds for you
- Where you are with each step
- Where you can improve as mentor or mentee
- How you can design meaningful experiences and learning for you both during each step

You might miss a move now and then, but in the end, you will step smartly along the path to mentoring success.

KNOW.

"Know where to find the information and
use it—that's the secret to success."
— ALBERT EINSTEIN

Step 1
KNOW.
– I Do –
Characteristics

The Mentor:

- Has learned the job well

- Is effective at performing the job

- Understands and can explain not only the how but the why

- Continually seeks to improve their skill set

- Finds a work-around for areas of weakness

- Seeks to share their skills and aptitudes with others

CHAPTER 26

How Shall I Mentor Thee?
Let Me Count the Ways—
By What I Do and Who I Am

Do what you can, with what you have, where you are."
— THEODORE ROOSEVELT

WHY WOULD ANYONE WANT YOU to be their mentor?
Is it because:

- You are networked better than Bill Gates, Mark Zuckerberg and Marissa Mayer combined?
- You are Clooney-esque in your suave, debonair manner and can win over any client?
- You can move an audience to tears with each scintillating quarterly operating report you deliver?
- You can design a complex widget with one hand tied behind your back and both eyes closed?
- You have the best golf handicap west of the Mississippi?

Make a mental list—what do you hope to impart to your mentee?

We know it is going to be different for each of you. (And mentees, you will likely be looking for different proficiencies in your chosen mentor.)

Mentors, you will mentor through what you know and do as well as through who you are.

- One mentee will want to learn a very specific skill you can teach.

- Another may learn to handle a tough team situation by observing your example.
- Another may need to see how a leader takes the high road when it would be easier to bend the rules.

Knowing what you are able to transfer and expressly what your mentee is looking for will avoid a conversation like this:

> Boss: "Amanda, I'd like you to mentor Joe. He badly needs a mentor."
> Amanda: "What shall I mentor him in?"
> Boss: "I don't know for sure. Just mentor him."

What? That's like shooting buckshot at a one-inch target a mile away. What is a mentor to do with that?

Here are five Powerful Proficiencies™ that a mentor can impart. You will benefit your mentee in one or many of these ways.

Powerful Proficiencies™

Pragmatics
You may have a very specific skill and your mentee will learn practical how-to expertise. You may mentor them to:

- Write software code
- Design a complex engineering solution
- Build a component on a factory line
- Analyze a financial document
- Deliver a tight, comprehensive presentation

Whatever the craft or skill, it is specific, with a beginning and an end and a completed product.

Passport
Your mentoring contribution comes largely through introductions and strengthening your mentee's network. You become a "Passporter" because:

- You know people that they don't

- You have access and influence
- You can call or text a strategic contact and the meeting will happen

In his book, *The Tipping Point*, Malcolm Gladwell describes these passporting leaders as connectors:

"Connectors are the people in a community who know large numbers of people and who are in the habit of making introductions. [They are] essentially the social equivalent of a computer network hub. They are people who 'link us up with the world…people with a special gift for bringing the world together.'"[26]

[They are] fantastic at expanding a mentee's network. They will say things like:

> "Oh you should talk to…"
> "Have you heard about…"
> "Let me introduce you to…"

They think in nodes, not individuals, and like nothing more than to help you.[27]

Every mentor can benefit a mentee by offering introductions and some of you will be especially gifted passporters.

Presence

I had a boss once who often complimented others by saying, "They command a presence." Translated, that meant the person had an air of authority and respect just by their presence in the room.

Many years ago, I owned two lovable but errant cocker spaniels. They had little respect for my commands and despite plying them with every kind of steak-flavored dog treat I could lay my hands on, when commanded to "sit," they would give me the animal version of "see ya later, baby!" and scamper off to a different part of the house.

I hired Brad, the trainer, to come to our house to educate them—and mostly me—on our turf. This next scenario drove me nuts. He would walk in the front door, say nothing other than "Hello" to me, look directly at the dogs and, no kidding, those two dogs would snap to attention, slam their behinds to the floor in a "sit" position and stare obediently up into his face. It was like the Dog King had entered the room.

Now that's the presence I'm talking about.

Funny isn't it? Some people have it and some don't but we know it when we see it.

Our brains are programmed to pay attention to whatever someone with a commanding presence says or does. It does not matter much if this person is your doctor, plumber, teacher, or president. Chances are, those who possess such presence have somehow earned it.[28] As a mentor, you may offer an impressive example of how to handle authority and command a presence.

Position

Oftentimes you are invited to mentor someone simply because of your business position.

I mentored a young man who told me he would walk by my office door and think, "I want that office someday. I want Lori's job." (There were some tough, exhausting days when I wanted to yell out the door, "Hey Brandon, over to you buddy, it's all yours!")

Your mentee might say, "I want to be an engineering director one day so I'd like to know what I need to do to get there." Your boss may say, "You are strong as a procurement manager, take on this mentee and show them the ropes."

The mentoring occurs often as a mentee is being groomed for the next step in business and is commonly seen at executive levels.

A technology company I know offers an internship position that allows the person to shadow the president for a year. The interns have many responsibilities, from managing the president's schedule to creating presentations for top executive meetings. Because of their potential, these interns are offered access to the hallowed halls of the executive's office.

I've often thought this would be an invaluable experience because the mentee gets quick exposure and insight into the company's inside scoop.

The mentee would receive answers to these questions:

- What is the real job description for this position?
- What other positions or departments do they interact with daily?
- What problems do they commonly encounter?
- How does the leader handle challenging office politics?

If you mentor because of your position, you will reveal your real job description played out in real life.

Passion

My mentor, Tom, was a passionate leader. It was amazing to see his zeal over a host of commitments and interests at work, home and in the community.

I watched Tom vigorously engage in exchanges with our CEO, his boss. I saw him speak boldly to our competitors. He self-assuredly presented his recommendations: "What? You don't buy into this plan? Let me demonstrate how we can make this a win-win."

At work, he stood his ground and came in every day with his shoulder to the wheel. He seemed to be one of those about whom the saying was coined, "Find a job that you love, and you'll never work a day in your life."

He was passionate about his home and family. He and his wife invited many of us over each year to watch his alma mater, Ohio State, compete in a College Bowl game (Ohio State usually entered the fray in some respect). We delighted in watching him and his three sons yell and vault over the furniture whenever the Buckeyes got a ref's call in their favor.

He reached out into the community, too. He taught a seventh-grade boys' Sunday school class at his church (he had to be an energetic soldier to take that on).

It was an honor to be mentored by a well-rounded individual who had well-rounded passions. Tom clearly shared his "deeper yes" burning inside.

You might find yourself mentoring because of your all-around life passions.

Which of these five powerful proficiencies do you relate to?

Which ones are you imparting now?

 Questions to Motivate MentorShift

1. As a mentor, which proficiencies do you most naturally offer?

2. As a mentee, from which of the Powerful Proficiencies would you most benefit?

3. As a mentor, is it possible to mentor in all proficiencies? Why or why not?

CHAPTER 27

Professional Mentors Not Required— What if I'm not an Expert?

"We are all experts in our own little niches."

— ALEX TREBEK, TELEVISION PERSONALITY

I've HAD MANY PEOPLE, young and old, say to me, "I'd love to mentor someone, but I'm not an expert in anything." They then go on to share their list of perceived limitations and personal doubts and I listen empathetically for a brief moment.

Quickly, I jump in and say, "You don't have to be an expert to mentor someone. You just need more experience and learning in an area than the person you are mentoring."

My son is learning to play the electric guitar. All it takes to transport him to rock heaven is to turn on the YouTube video of Eddie Van Halen playing "Jump," and his face lights up. He is mesmerized by Van Halen's guitar licks and joy in playing.

After watching the video for the umpteenth time, his eyes have a faraway look and he says, "What if Eddie Van Halen would teach me to play like that?" He wishes Eddie would walk into our living room carrying his EVH Wolfgang Special guitar.

Eddie is likely busy with concert tours so the chances are slim.

On the other hand, Mitch, my son's guitar teacher, impacts my son's life in a powerful way.

Mitch has taught him to run scales, improvise and play cool guitar riffs. He is an excellent musician, patiently instructs students each week and pursues ways to improve his own skills, making him an effective Step 1 mentor.

While you may have always thought that a great mentor had to be an absolute expert, I offer an emphatic "No!"

My son may be inspired to rock star status by Eddie Van Halen, but he will put fingers to the guitar and launch his own career through the model and encouragement of his mentor, Mitch.

A Step 1 mentor exhibits these first three qualifications:

- Has learned the job well
- Is effective at performing the job
- Understands and can explain not only the how but the why

Sometimes I hear early career individuals say that since they haven't been in the workforce for long, they aren't qualified to mentor.

But they should remember, they don't have to be experts to mentor. They just need more experience and learning in some area than the person they are mentoring.

Let's check out Aaron, an early career employee, who is on his way to accomplishing Step 1 – I Do mentoring skills.

Has learned the job well

Aaron had worked in advertising for a couple of years. During that time, he would frequently think, "I'm going to make hay while the sun shines." He knew that he had a great opportunity to learn from a team of strong advertising whizzes in his firm and he took advantage of that.

He asked his bosses a lot of questions and joined Google+ circles to exchange knowledge with his peers. Even though he was only on the job two years, he developed a solid knowledge base and was quickly acquiring experience.

Is effective at performing the job

Aaron took the time to master many advertising software interactive applications and took part in Internet advertising competitions.

He regularly presented convincing ideas and concepts to his clients.

He also asked bigger, more strategic questions like, "What are the future trends and issues that could influence the advertising industry?" and "How can we use lean start-up techniques to reach our consumers?"

He became known around his department as a go-to guy.

Understands and can explain not only the *how* but the *why*

If you overheard Aaron explaining an idea to a colleague, you might hear him saying, "We use interactive marketing in these cases because our audiences' average time spent on-site justifies it."

Or, "For a new company, pairing it with a high traffic business is a great plan. If we're selling shoes, we'll put a kiosk in an airport or mall where people are walking, because then we'll have immediate access to the right market."

Aaron has learned not only an effective way to produce good work but *why* those ways work.

Looking at Aaron's skill base and experience, he is clearly a Step 1 – I Do mentor-to-be. When Jake joins the firm and is just learning the ropes, Mitch is ready to step in and show him those ropes.

Aaron is not an expert yet but he will be an outstanding mentor.

If you're learning new skills to teach others—great! Singer-songwriter John Mayer said, "If you had started doing anything two weeks ago, by today you would have been two weeks better at it." Start now and soon you'll be ready to show others.

If you have been in your line of work for many years, then you have even more in-depth strategies and wisdom to pass on.

Where are you strong? What can you pass on?

You need to find out.

In the words of Van Halen, "Go ahead, you might as well jump!"

Questions to Motivate MentorShift

1. What skills or position do you "know well?"

2. Why is it important to be able to explain not only the how but the why when mentoring others?

3. Give an example of someone you know like Mitch, the guitar teacher, who is a strong Step 1 mentor. Describe their characteristics.

CHAPTER 28

Pump up your Mentoring Muscles— Mentor from your Strengths

"The greatest room for each person's growth is in the areas of his greatest strength."

— DONALD O. CLIFTON, BUSINESS AUTHOR

EVERYONE IS A 10 in some area.

Do you believe that?

Marcus Buckingham and Donald Clifton do.

In their bestseller, *Now, Discover Your Strengths*, they identify 34 areas of strength that they believe people exhibit; everything from responsibility to focus to woo (the ability to win over others).

The authors assert that everyone has at least one skill they can perform better than the next 10,000 others. That means they believe everyone can be a 10 in some area.[29]

I suppose it depends on your definition of a 10, but I would say that each of us has at least one pretty robust 8 or 9 area of strength that can be our mentoring springboard.

The problem is that we often don't really have that strength well identified.

What about you? Do you know where you are strong?

I often have people say to me, "I don't know what I'm really good at, I just know what I like to do."

Excellent. I immediately respond, "Tell me more about what you *like* to do. What do others say you are good at doing?"

I've heard some of the following replies:

> "I'm good at troubleshooting mechanical problems."
> "I can put together an impressive presentation."
> "I know how to leverage social media in marketing."
> "It's easy for me to analyze financial statements."
> "I do a great job helping new employees learn a new task."

Tony Robbins, author of *Awaken the Giant Within*, said it very well, "It's not knowing what to do, it's doing what you know."

We each have areas that we know and where we shine.

These strengths could be qualities about ourselves that we have known for as long as we can remember. They may be areas that others have consistently complimented or congratulated us on.

They are talents that have not only an "I can't help it" quality to them but also an "it feels good" quality.[30]

For Ryan, all his life his strength has been public speaking.

At six years old, he recited a portion of Hamlet's Soliloquy in his school play. In high school, his teachers prodded him to go into debate and public speaking. In business, no matter what the rest of his annual rating said, the "effective presentations" block consistently received a happy smiling face.

If you handed him a script or needed an impromptu presentation, he would jump to his feet.

Guess how he decided to mentor someone? In public speaking!

We all have these jump-to-our-feet abilities.

What would you jump to your feet about?

Lida Citroen, author of *Reputation 360: Creating Power through Personal Branding*, framed it another way when she asked me, "Lori, when was a time that you were doing something that really felt like a rock star moment to you?"

What a great question!

I had once presented a message to a group of early career leadership development program applicants. They were eager to join the fast-track program and advance their careers.

I was even more eager to draw them higher, to a point where they achieved stunning careers but also celebrated others' accomplishments. I urged them to give back by mentoring right from the get-go and make their careers something that mattered.

After the speech one of the attendees, Matthew, literally chased me down the hall. With emotion in his voice, he said, "The kind of person you were talking about—that is who I want to be."

Kioko stood behind him, misty-eyed, waiting to share the same news. Zach waited also.

As I walked to the parking lot, I was grinning ear-to-ear. I knew during and after that speech that I was in my zone. From then on, I never wanted to only instruct or motivate about mentoring—I wanted to *inspire* others to mentor.

When did you experience a rock star moment?

The message is clear—know your strengths and invest in others through them.

Achieving Step 1 – I Do requires that...

- You know where your strengths and talents lie
- You know where you can best contribute from your experience
- You know you can be confident in those abilities

This is an important first step to becoming an effective mentor.

In order to be a mentor, you need to have identified where you can mentor well.

Invest some time to evaluate your talents and strengths. Do three quick inventories. Write them down.

- Things I Like to Do
- Things Others Have Said I Do Well
- My Rock Star Moments

Perhaps you even want to take a personal inventory such as Tom Rath's StrengthsFinder 2.0[31] or the Leadership Skills Inventory.[32]

Any of these efforts will help you identify where you might need to sharpen your skills or where you are ready to jump to your feet now.

Questions to Motivate MentorShift

1. What areas cause you to jump to your feet, knowing you are strong and could teach someone else?

2. Do you recall a rock star moment? What was it like? How did you know that you were in your zone?

3. How confident are you in your ability to pass on skills in your strength area?

CHAPTER 29

The Confident Mentor— Shoring up your Savvy

"Confidence is going after Moby Dick in a rowboat and taking the tartar sauce with you."

— ZIG ZIGLAR, MOTIVATIONAL SPEAKER

WHAT'S THE BIGGEST DIFFERENCE between James Bond and Charlie Brown (besides cool cars, adventure, awesome spy gadgets and stunning women)?

It's confidence.

For 50 years, Bond has uttered in his cool, inimitable way, "Bond. James Bond." No one delivers it quite like he does.

Charlie, on the other hand, says, "If I stand here, I can see the little red-haired girl when she comes out of her house…of course, if she sees me peeking around this tree, she'll think I'm the dumbest person in the world…but if I don't peek around the tree, I'll never see her…which means I probably AM the dumbest person in the world…which explains why I'm standing in a batch of poison oak."[33]

There's quite a chasm of confidence between the two, isn't there?

When it comes to mentoring, I know I've felt composed and on top of my game at times and like I was standing in a batch of poison oak at others.

I've also been somewhere in between.

How's your confidence level when it comes to mentoring?

We know we don't need to be experts to mentor and that we will mentor most effectively through our strengths.

Now it's a matter of stepping out confidently.

As you are becoming a Step 1 – I Do mentor, there are three important things to do to build your confidence and ability, both for beginning as well as seasoned mentors.

A confident mentor exhibits these second three Step 1 qualifications:

- Continually seeks to improve their skill set
- Finds a work-around for areas of weakness
- Consistently seeks to share their skills and aptitudes with others

Let's look more closely at each of these characteristics.

Continually seeks to improve their skill set

First, although we might excel at what we do, we can always do better and learn more. (Even renowned Renaissance artist, Michelangelo, at the ripe age of 87, famously said, "I'm still learning.")

How can you continue to improve your craft?

There's a wide spectrum of opportunities to grow in your strength areas.

- Individual research
- Online classes
- Company offered classes
- Offsite workshops
- Shadowing
- Stretch assignment
- Regular performance feedback

What actions to improve your skill set would make you a more confident, effective mentor?

Find a work-around for areas of weakness

In the last chapter we focused on the value of mentoring from our strengths. We should note, sometimes we spend time tirelessly working on our weaknesses and attempting to mentor from those areas.

What happens? Frustration.

Amy, for example, is a gifted electrical engineer. She troubleshoots problems quickly and her technical solutions move the engineering process along. However, she is not strong in envisioning markets for her product and strategically planning the five-year product line.

How would you prefer Amy to mentor you—in strategic planning or in technical problem solving?

Of course it would be in technical problem solving where she is strong.

If she sought to help you learn strategic planning you would both likely end up feeling frustrated.

John Maxwell, in his book *Mentoring 101*, offers an interesting thought about improving on our weaknesses:

> "When it comes to improving skills, I believe that most people cannot increase their ability beyond about two points on a scale of 1 to 10. So for example, if you were born a 4 when it comes to math, no matter how hard you work at it, you will probably never become better than a 6. But here's the good news. Everybody is exceptional at something, and a 10 doesn't always look the same."[34]

Do you agree with Mr. Maxwell?

I do. I believe that investing energy and effort on areas where you may never really shine may not pay off. I do believe, though, that you can develop a strategic work-around to excel in your weaker areas and this will bolster confidence.

I offer a personal example about the years I spent in the financial arena.

Looking back, I was a bit of a right-brained girl in a left-brained world when it came to the complex mathematical parts of my job. I liked math and did well in it, but preferred to lead a team through the messiness of a tough project. (I worked alongside many math Einsteins, though, whose eyes would sparkle at the thought of logistical regressions and hyperbolic curves!)

I worked mergers and acquisitions and knew that what I really loved was helping two fierce business rivals play well together on the playground. I enjoyed building the bridges between competing companies to create maximum value for the shareholders.

While I advanced through leadership positions, I found the most success when I worked to my strengths—team building, project management, communication—and surrounded myself with mathematical technical experts.

In any acquisition deal, the financial forecast critically guides the decision path. I was able to revel in the challenge of those endeavors by utilizing the support of excellent mathematical analysts.

That way I could lead through my strengths.

Consistently seeks to share their skills and aptitudes with others

A confident mentor practices sharing their skills. Howard was such an employee.

White-haired and bespectacled, we had nicknamed him "The Professor." He had been with the company for 40 years and considered the workplace his classroom. He was content with his position as a senior analyst as long as he was able to teach others and help them become successful.

Each time new employees were hired into the company, they somehow gravitated to Howard. It seemed he had an invisible welcome sign hung on his cubicle wall.

Howard was always practicing his mentoring and by so doing, he left a lot of fellow employees better off than they were before they met him.

He was a confident mentor and that confidence had developed through one thing—practice, practice, practice. He continually looked for ways to share his skills with others.

Criss Jami, in his book *Venus in Arms*, shares an observation about developing confidence: "Confidence is like a dragon where, for every head cut off, two more heads grow back."[35]

It's a funny illustration, but true. The more you practice sharing your skills and aptitudes, the more you will grow your mentoring self-assurance.

Improve your skill set, find work-arounds, practice sharing your skills and aptitudes.

Chances are, by claiming these three characteristics as your own, you can become, in the spirit of Mr. Bond—"Mentor, Confident Mentor."

Questions to Motivate MentorShift

1. Do you feel confident in mentoring someone else? If so, why do you feel that way? If not, how might you shore up your savvy?

2. What are some specific ways you can continue to perfect your skill set?

3. How might you develop a work-around in your weaker area?

Summary
Step 1
KNOW.
– I Do –

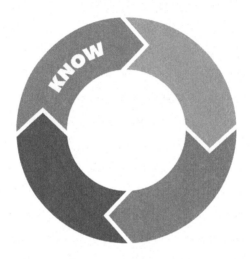

The Mentor:

- Has learned the job well

- Is effective at performing the job

- Understands and can explain not only the how but the why

- Continually seeks to improve their skill set

- Finds a work-around for areas of weaknesses

- Seeks to share their skills and aptitudes with others

SECTION 4

SHOW.

"Don't tell me the moon is shining; show me the glint of light on broken glass."

— ANTON CHEKHOV, MASTER STORYTELLER

141

Step 2
SHOW.
– I Do, You Contribute –
Characteristics

- Mentor and mentee plan events and activities for the mentee to observe

- Mentor performs tasks and skills as the mentee observes

- Mentor explains how and why as they go along

- Mentee asks questions throughout time with the mentor

- Mentee contributes to the activity to strengthen learning

CHAPTER 30

The Power of "With"

"God, send me anywhere, only go with me."
DR. DAVID LIVINGSTONE, FAMED EXPLORER AND MEDICAL MISSIONARY

WHY DOES A HUSBAND want to be with his wife in the delivery room? (No, it's not just because he'd pay dearly if he weren't there!) Why does a mother want to be with her baby to see his first step?

Why does a lovestruck guy want to be with the girl of his dreams every minute of every hour?

Are you catching the operative word?

WITH.

It's a small but powerful word. It's just a lonely little preposition like "by, through, under, over and around." It means "to accompany, be in some particular relation to, implying connection."[36]

It's clear-cut and direct—a little four-letter, insignificant preposition. Or is it?

Think of the meaningful experiences of our personal lives, the ones that define each one of us in relationship to the world around us.

A young boy beams, "I was *with* my dad when I caught my first fish. It was a whopper and he helped me do it!"

A college student shares, "I was *with* my best friend when we ran our first half marathon. I don't think I could have made it the whole way without her."

In our business lives, the same holds true.

> A new manager exclaims, "My boss took me *with* her when we cut the deal. I watched the whole negotiation and saw how she led us to a great outcome."

> A promising analyst shares, "I was *with* my team 24-7 when we wrote the proposal. It took us three months but we put together an outstanding bid."

There is something precious, almost noble, about life as it happens when we are *with* those we care about and *with* those we mentor.

We can't imagine any of the above scenarios really being accomplished by an articulate, professional e-mail or an arms-length, hour-long meeting.

If we're honest with ourselves, we yearn to be there to be a part of whatever is happening so we can take in the experience alongside the person who is our loved one, friend, mentor or mentee.

In one workplace example, my colleagues and I knew being with our boss would bring learning and rewards. Many times we toiled into the wee hours of the night on a presentation to our senior leaders. Because we were junior employees, we were not invited to attend the meeting itself but we had done a lot of the work. When our boss would return from the meeting we'd all clamor to find out every detail. We would eagerly ask, "So, how did it go?"

When he would just respond, "Better than expected, thanks," we would quietly feel a letdown. *If only* we could have heard what was being said and seen how he fielded the questions. *If only* we'd been there to feel the tension in the room over that certain issue-of-the-day and hear how it was resolved.

It would have been great to be there with him.

MentorShift is about "with-mentoring." I want to plant that seed early and plant it deep so that it takes root and grows in your mind as you read on.

Mentors, be someone who purposes to be *with* your mentee. Mentees, ask your mentors to go *with* them.

A while back I held a workshop on the four-step MentorShift process for a group of high potential professionals. I ended my presentation saying, "If you remember nothing else that I shared with you today, remember the power of 'with.'"

A few months later at a holiday party in a friend's home, a young woman approached me and said, "I remember you from the MentorShift presentation you gave to our group. I wanted to tell you how much being a 'with-mentor' has transformed mentoring for me. It's crazy because it was a pretty simple change to do and it made a big impact. I invite my mentees to go with me so often now."

That was gratifying to hear and underscored, once again, the power of "with."

We'll look further into the specifics of how to leverage with-mentoring in your relationships. For now, let's dig a little deeper into another example of what with-mentoring looks like.

 Questions to Motivate MentorShift

1. What was the last great life experience you had *with* someone? (PG-13 please!)

2. What was the last great work experience you had when someone invited you to go with them? Why did it benefit you?

3. Does a "with-mentor" jump to your mind? If so, who are they and what did they do?

CHAPTER 31

The Power of "Share by Showing"— Real Cowboys Get Their Boots Dirty

"Would you go with me as we roll down streets of fire?"
— JOSH TAYLOR, FROM HIS COUNTRY HIT, "WOULD YOU GO WITH ME?"

I'M A COWBOY'S DAUGHTER straight from the heart of Nebraska. My dad, grandfather and great grandfather were all in the cattle business. I knew this early on by what we ate for dinner every night. I never had to ask, "Where's the beef?"

But my appreciation of the cattle business was about far more than dinner.

From as early as I can remember, my dad would take my brother and me out on the open road and would show us what the cattle business was about. We'd jostle along on the bumpy pastures to get right up close to the grazing cattle. Dad would start the inevitable quiz. He'd say, "Which is an Angus, a Hereford, a Long Horn? Would that steer make it to market?"

Trivial Pursuit really should have a category for Cattle Facts—I'd be a tough competitor.

Dad and Grandpa also took many young cowboys with them as they traveled those dusty roads. The key word is *with* them. They took the young cowboys with them to round up the cattle and to strike a deal. They believed that if those young men didn't "look the critter in the face" and "get their boots dirty" too, they weren't really learning the business. *They rarely worked alone.*

So what do bumpy cattle pastures have to do with a book on mentoring? My dad and grandpa gave me a clear example of great mentoring that I still use today.

Mentoring was not a textbook experience, it was a hands-on life experience.

You learned by going *with* them. They shared the process by showing how it's done.

You might be thinking, "But a cowboy life lends itself easily to Share by Showing mentoring. How can they judge a steer's weight unless they are actually there? How can they close the deal unless they are at the negotiation table together? The mentee *has* to go along with the mentor to help them learn the task. It's totally different in my business world today!"

But is it? I'd offer an emphatic no! Although we all work virtually and are accustomed to the challenges that cross-cultural environments and differing time zones present, the same holds true in the business world. For the most effective mentoring, we need to go *with*. See it firsthand. Observe our mentors in action. (We'll talk more about how to address the challenges that distance brings later in this section.)

In business today, we've defaulted to a couple of less than satisfactory models.

I've interviewed dozens of my colleagues and experts in the business world because I've wanted to learn what's out there in terms of mentoring practices today. I have come away with a couple of common ways of doing mentoring business.

In essence, this first mentoring practice conveys, "Mentoring = A Methodical Meeting." You might find yourself in a structured, formal set-up that is time-bound and guided by a book or program. This can lead to the problem expressed by Sandra Wiley (ranked in the top 100 most influential accounting professionals), "The problem with mentor programs is that they are often canned, and the current leaders in the firm will not make the necessary commitment to ensure the program works."[37]

In this instance, your company may have paired you with a mentor/ mentee and both of you have recorded the mentoring set-up as part of your annual performance goals. ("Whew, now I can check that box!")

Because mentoring happens in the office for a determined timeframe, commonly the mentee shares their problem du jour and the mentor responds with a version of, "Here is what I did way back when." The mentee then leaves the office and dutifully promises to return in a set amount of time.

It's pretty formal and *not very flexible*.

Sound familiar?

In the second example, you share your cubicle wall with Bob or Bella or Rick or Rachel and they know something about what you want to learn. So, through hanging out over the cubicle wall and hoping for the kindness of a fellow worker, you pick up the skill you are seeking through their goodwill to you. It's peer-to-peer mentoring at its most informal. (This is the mentoring style commonly found in small businesses. There are fewer barriers to this informal communication and they often lack the budgets to support a full mentoring program.)

A senior corporate colleague and former vice president of human resources told me, "Mentoring can be luck of the draw. If you happen to sit next to someone that can help you learn something, they might become your ad hoc mentor and you are darn *lucky*." Here, mentoring is very informal and somewhat happenstance.

Both mentoring models have their merits because relationships are being built. But they are a far cry from a 'with-mentoring' and 'share by showing' approach.

Take heart—there is a better way.

When you take your mentees with you and Share by Showing, you directly reinforce *how they learn*, that is, socially, emotionally and physiologically. You'll see more about why showing and observing is such a powerful learning method in the next chapters.

Share by Showing mentoring has an element of "stretch" in the business world. We have to be *intentional* and *creative* because we do spend the majority of our time in our offices.

Recently, after I'd conducted a mentoring seminar, Ben, a president of his own software company pulled me aside. He was clearly bothered and he said,

"I've got some trouble in my company right now. My employees' morale is not what it used to be. I've also just had two key contributors leave the company."

I replied, "Ben, what are your thoughts as to why this is happening?"

He went on, "After listening to your 'with' idea, I realize I've been taking the easy way out lately. I used to say to those I was mentoring, 'Come hang out with me in my office. Listen to me as I discuss situations on the phone and conduct various meetings. Just watch and learn. Then we can talk about it afterwards.'"

I said, "That sounds pretty healthy. You were giving your team a chance to be in on what was going on."

He continued, "Well, I've quit doing that. The past few months I've just dumped tasks on my mentees and left it at that. Inviting them into my world is a lot more work, it's an investment, you know."

"An investment that has some payoffs?" I asked.

He smiled knowingly and replied, "Lots of payoffs. I'd lost my commitment to have them with me and show them what I'm doing. I want to get back to the way I did it before."

Ben was right to return to his former ways. He's an intuitive leader and knows that meaningful, fun and transformational things can happen when we are with someone.

I connected with Ben recently and he shared, "Life is much better! I opened up my office door again and started inviting some of the gang to join me in whatever I was doing that day.

"I am still working the retention issue but I can tell morale is improving. Bringing the team with me is such a better way to go."

When you mentor, do you share by showing?

 ## Questions to Motivate MentorShift

1. Where and when do you most commonly mentor?

2. Why would it be important to be a Share by Showing mentor? What are the clear benefits to both mentor and mentee?

3. Where might you next invite your mentee to go with you? Where might you ask your mentor to go with them? Be specific.

CHAPTER 32

The Power of Watching Your Mentor— Poor Ol' Bobo and the Social Learning Experiment

"You can observe a lot just by watching."

— YOGI BERRA, BASEBALL HALL OF FAMER

HAVE YOU EVER HEARD OF Albert Bandura's Bobo Doll? He was an inflatable, bounce-back clown that got the living daylights whacked out of him.

Now, that sounds like an unfortunate consequence for a harmless, smiling clown but his sacrifice did much to further an understanding of how people learn.

Social psychologist Albert Bandura put forward a theory he called observational learning, or social learning. Simply put, the idea was that individuals can learn new information and behaviors simply by watching someone else do something and observing the consequences of their behavior.

Enter our star, Bobo. In Bandura's famous Bobo Doll experiment, he set about to study how daycare center children would respond after observing an adult model punching, kicking and yelling at the Bobo Doll.

Sometimes the adult was rewarded for their behavior, other times punished. After watching this, the children were put in the testing room with the Bobo Doll and their actions observed.

Bandura found the children were more likely to imitate the adult model by pummeling poor Bobo if:

- They had *observed* the aggressive behavior (versus a control group of children that didn't observe it)
- The adult was an attractive, authority figure
- The adult was positively reinforced afterwards

He also found that if the adult model was negatively reinforced (punished) the children were less likely to imitate them, suggesting that:

- A step of reasoning had entered in ("Oh no, she got in trouble for hitting the clown.")
- They weighed the potential negative consequences ("I might get in trouble too.")
- They could choose *not* to imitate ("I'm not going to hit that clown.")

We are social creatures and not unlike the kids in the Bandura experiment. We observe others' actions and then we make a judgment—do I want to do what they did or not?

Observational learning has *big* implications when it comes to mentoring.

Why? Because it is likely that your mentor fits Bandura's criteria of being an attractive individual you observe often who is positively reinforced for their work behavior and ethic.

You are likely to be keenly influenced by a model like that and you will choose whether or not you wish to imitate them.

Just like the kids in the Bobo experiment, you have that step of cognition...that moment of pause when your inner voice asks, "Wait, is this behavior something I want to do myself?"

Earlier, I related the story of my father who impacted young cowboys' lives through his patient, consistent "with" mentoring. He was rewarded for that behavior by the way they caught on to the business and the respect with which they regarded him.

I purposed to copy that behavior with the individuals I have mentored since then.

Alternatively, in the early days of my industry career, I witnessed some bad behavior on the part of those I looked up to. I call them the "cussers and chairkickers" because they routinely handled conflict with coarse demonstrations of dressing others down in public. It seemed to be a part of the culture at that time.

Eventually, those leaders were negatively reinforced for that behavior by loss of respect, loss of promotional opportunity and in some cases, termination from their positions.

I decided early on that I didn't want to be like them.

What was similar between my observations of my dad and observations of the badly behaving leaders?

I watched both role models and their images were clear in my mind. What was different?

I opted to emulate one and not the other.

A great tip? *Mentees—Choose your mentors well so that you might observe (generally) positive and constructive behaviors.*

Observational learning won't have to center around mentors punching and whooping on inanimate objects (a clown can only take so much) but rather on observing positive role models who:

- Lead productive meetings
- Give honest, helpful feedback
- Present valuable data to management
- Admit their mistakes and correct them
- Show a genuine interest in you

That's the kind of behavior you want to observe.

The first two elements of Step 2 – I Do, You Contribute are as follows:

- Mentor and mentee plan events and activities for the mentee to observe
- Mentor performs tasks and skills while the mentee observes

When others watch you, what do they see?

Questions to Motivate MentorShift

1. Who is someone in your workplace that you observe frequently? What behaviors of theirs have you observed repeatedly?

2. Think of a time when you have watched someone be rewarded for their actions. What was your response? Think of a time when someone was negatively reinforced. What was your reaction to that?

3. Why do you think observational learning is such a foundational part of mentoring?

CHAPTER 33

The Power of Example— "Be Like Mike"

"Few things are harder to put up with than the annoyance of a good example."

— MARK TWAIN, AUTHOR AND HUMORIST

REMEMBER THE CATCHY pitch song for Gatorade—*Be Like Mike?* "Sometimes I dream that he is me…I wanna be like Mike."

These were unforgettable commercials. Exuberant children, feel-good-all-over footage of M.J.'s massive slam dunks and rivers of neon-colored Gatorade for everyone.

It's cool to be like someone who is cool, wouldn't you agree?

People generally desire association with things that are cool, exciting, dynamic, and culturally relevant. Michael Jordan and his highlights were all of these things.[38]

It's hard to argue M.J.'s stratospheric prowess on the court, but whether it was men's fashion or even his questionable affinity for gambling, Michael Jordan cast a long shadow. People watched what Michael would do and he knew it.

People watch what you do, are you aware of that? Mentor—that's especially true of your mentee.

For our purposes, let's climb down from the world of 10-foot regulation hoops to the solid ground and talk about example.

Your example.

What's the definition of example? It's "a person, action, thing, etc., that is worthy of imitation; a pattern."[39]

Is your example worthy of imitation?

155

There are a million ways to set a positive example. I've chosen two essential traits of 'real deal' mentors that demonstrate the power of inspiring example.

Integrity

We're always impressed when we see someone do the right thing. Your co-worker says, "That was my error. I will correct it now and it won't happen again." She could have let it slide and let you take the fall but she didn't.

Even more noteworthy is the person who sets an example by doing the right thing and possibly going unnoticed. Author C.S. Lewis said, "Integrity is doing the right thing, even when no one is watching."

Brennan was a good example of that. He was a guy who could become really annoying to his less charitable fellow workers—and not because of his work habits or an eccentric mannerism. It was because he wouldn't take part in the office gossip.

He had a unique way of changing the subject when something bad came up about someone not present. Once an individual raised the subject of Jessie and her perceived lack of ability at her job. I recall Brennan saying, "Jessie has a son my son's age. He's a really good basketball player, they play together on the same team." He diverted the topic to something positive.

At other times, he would look quietly down and not comment. More often than not, he'd say, "I haven't had that same experience with them. That's hard for me to comment on. Why don't you just go ask them about it."

That usually stopped the gossip in its tracks.

He continually reminded me of Stephen Covey's teaching, "If you want to retain those who are present, be loyal to those who are absent because the key to the many is the one."

Brennan did the right thing when no one was watching. Sure, others saw his reluctance to badmouth someone. But more importantly, Brennan guarded other peoples' reputations when they weren't there to represent themselves. That person often never knew that he stood up for them in their absence.

(The rest of the office did.)

Respect/Kindness

In the book, *Harry Potter and the Goblet of Fire*, Sirius Black says, "If you want to know what a man's like, take a good look at how he treats his inferiors, not his equals."[40]

Sometimes "inferiors" are not that at all but rather people whom others put aside by dismissing their presence, importance or contribution. I saw an inspiring demonstration of respect and kindness in such a case through my own mother.

Besides being an irreplaceable mentor (and in the Mom Hall of Fame in my book), my mother is an R.N. who has specialized in Alzheimer's care. I never could really understand how she could enter that world of individuals who could not connect with the reality that I experienced.

I often would not go to the Alzheimer's home where she worked due to my own hesitation and discomfort. I didn't know what to say to the people who didn't know what to say to me.

One late evening, I picked my mother up from work. In the nursing home veranda, an older woman sat, looking expectantly out at the driveway. "I'm waiting for my husband to pick me up, he usually comes about this time."

My mom replied, "Vera, I'd only wait about 10 more minutes and then go on to bed. We've waited for a while and something must have come up."

Vera's husband had passed away 20 years before.

Vera wanted to wait just a little longer. Mom let her do that and came back to check. She helped her off to bed with comforting words about tomorrow.

There was another woman in the facility who had raised twin girls. In her mind, she was still a brand-new mother with her babies on her knee. My mother gave her two baby dolls and talked with her about her girls and helped her wrap them up in blankets.

The woman was so grateful. Finally, someone who understood how important it was to keep a newborn warm. She was at peace as she held the two dolls.

I sat wide-eyed as I watched Mom in these situations. She treated these dear ones with respect and kindness that came as second nature to her.

Mom would say, "They might not have their memory but they deserve to be understood and treated with dignity."

She could have given me dozens of lessons on Alzheimer's care or books to read, but nothing would have touched my mind and heart like watching her example. It sculpted compassion and care into my heart in a lasting way.

Nobel Peace Prize winner Albert Schweitzer said, "Example is not the main thing in influencing others, it is the only thing."

In your life, if you want to feel like the skies have opened and poured a waterfall of opportunity onto your lap, you can do the following:

You can use your life to be a good example…a *great* example to someone else.

It's a mentoring opportunity no one can ever take away from you. What will your example be?

 Questions to Motivate MentorShift

1. Whose life and actions have been a meaningful example to you? Why?

2. Besides integrity and impartiality, what other character traits can be modeled to others?

3. When you've observed the good example of a mentor, were you compelled to imitate it? Give an illustration.

CHAPTER 34

The Power of Imitation—
Phil Mickelson Is Not Really a Lefty

"I've been imitated so well I've heard people copy my mistakes."
— JIMI HENDRIX, ROCK MUSICIAN

CHAMPION GOLFER Phil Mickelson, Jr. began hitting golf balls when he was 18 months old.

Phil Sr. began to teach his toddler son the rudiments of swinging the golf club when the boy was physically able to stand without wobbling, hold a club and copy what his dad was doing.

Little Phil would stand opposite his dad, observe him and imitate his swing. His dad, a right-hander, would swing right to left—Little Phil would swing left to right. It was like he was looking in a mirror.

The game of golf ended up with Phil Mickelson, a left-handed hitter and arguably the game's best ever lefty—who is right-handed in *everything else*.[41]

What do you call that phenomenon?

The power of imitation.

What causes people to imitate others?

We've covered two significant reasons together so far.

The first is **social**. Through observational learning, you watch your mentor, judge the positive or negative responses they receive and determine if you want to do what they do. Social learning influences imitation, as we just read about in the Bobo experiment.

Secondly, you saw that you are drawn to be like someone who seems "cool" to you—someone whose character, style and choices you admire.

Those are more **emotional** or **intellectual** reasons, as in the case of so many people who emulated Michael Jordan.

There is a third and equally powerful influence that causes imitation and it is **physiological**. Powerful things happen in your brain when you observe your mentors.

James Zull, in his book, *The Art of the Changing Brain—Enriching the Practice of Teaching by Exploring the Biology of Learning,* confirms this potent influence when he states, "I had always believed that the brain operates by physical and chemical laws, and thus, that *learning is physical.*" Zull goes on "As new and different networks of neurons fire because of our sensory input—our experience—these networks constantly change. They form new connections and lose others. The brain physically changes.[42]

It's very important to realize what happens when we observe someone's actions. Our brains change to encode the new information—and they engage as if we were actually the one performing the actions.

Many scientists today believe mirror neurons are a significant cause of this.

In 1992, on a hot summer day in Parma, Italy, a monkey sat in a special laboratory chair waiting for researchers to return from lunch. Thin wires had been implanted in the region of its brain involved in planning and carrying out movements.

Every time the monkey grasped and moved an object, some cells in that brain region would fire, and a monitor would register a sound: brrrrrip, brrrrrip, brrrrrip.

A graduate student entered the lab with an ice cream cone in his hand. The monkey stared at him. Then, something amazing happened: When the student raised the cone to his lips, the monitor sounded—brrrrrip, brrrrrip, brrrrrip—even though the monkey had not moved *but had simply observed the student* grasping the cone and moving it to his mouth.

The researchers, led by Giacomo Rizzolatti, a neuroscientist at the University of Parma, had earlier noticed the same strange phenomenon with peanuts. The same brain cells fired when the monkey watched humans or other monkeys bring peanuts to their mouths as when the monkey itself brought a peanut to its mouth.

Later, the scientists found cells that fired when the monkey broke open a peanut or heard someone break a peanut. The same thing happened with bananas, raisins and all kinds of other objects.

"It took us several years to believe what we were seeing," Dr. Rizzolatti said in a recent interview. The monkey brain contains a special class of cells, called mirror neurons, that fire when the animal sees or hears an action and when the animal carries out the same action on its own.

But if the findings, published in 1996, surprised most scientists, recent research has left them flabbergasted. Humans, it turns out, have mirror neurons that are far smarter, more flexible and more highly evolved than any of those found in monkeys, a fact that scientists say reflects the evolution of humans' sophisticated social abilities.[43]

Hmmmm. So you watch your mentor deliver a rousing presentation. She is articulate and in command and persuades her audience. As you watch, you almost feel your adrenalin flowing. You practically feel as if it's you up there at the front of the room. You could do what she is doing.

That's your mirror neurons at work.

Dr. V.S. Ramachandran, neuroscientist at UC San Diego, further describes the concept, "Here's a neuron that fires when I reach and grab something, but it also fires when I watch Joe reach and grab for something. This is truly astonishing because it's as though this neuron is adopting the other person's point of view, like a virtual reality simulation of the other person's actions.

"What's the significance of these mirror neurons? They must be involved in imitation and emulation, because to imitate a complex action, it requires me to adopt the other person's point of view.[44]

"When mirror neurons are working correctly they fire both for doing an action and seeing the same action. This allows people to connect at a very simple level. Healthy humans are very social. What makes humans unique? [One thing] is culture which comes from imitation, watching your teachers do something."[45]

Daniel Glaser, University College London shares, "The mirror neuron is a big part of what makes us human. There'd be very little point of having a mirror system if you lived on your own. There would be a lot of point to having a digestive, movement or visual system if you lived on your own. But there'd be no point in having a mirror system.

"The mirror system is the most basic social brain system. There's no point in having it if you don't want to attract and relate to other people."[46]

Mentoring and mirror neurons? They are intimately connected because what you observe your mentor doing has powerful, engaging consequences in your brain.

Oliver Wendell Holmes said, "Once we stretch our mind around a new idea, it never returns to its former shape."

I'd submit that once we stretch our mind around a new sight or observation, it never returns to its former shape.

 ## Questions to Motivate MentorShift

1. What did you learn about the impact of mirror neurons to your learning?

2. How does knowledge of the physiological part of learning impact your choice of a mentor?

3. As a mentor, others will be imitating you. What specifically do you want them to observe and imitate?

CHAPTER 35

The Power of Memory—
The Giant Sticky Note
We Call our Brain

*"I always have trouble remembering three things: faces, names,
and—I can't remember what the third thing is."*

— FRED ALLEN, RADIO PERSONALITY

IN HIS BOOK, *Outliers,* Malcolm Gladwell repeatedly makes reference to the 10,000-Hour Rule.[47] He asserts that the key to success in any field is, to a great extent, a matter of practicing a specific task for a total of around 10,000 hours.

Yo Yo Ma, arguably the world's greatest cellist, has outdone this rule. He is reported to have practiced 50,000 hours in his illustrious career and life.[48]

Go to YouTube and watch him perform Saint Saens' *The Swan.*[49] He plays effortlessly, majestically, never looking at any music or his instrument. Instead he watches a street dancer and seems to be musing as he observes how the boy dances to the music.

His music is in his head. If you've practiced 50,000 hours, this probably isn't a big stretch.

You've heard the saying, "Practice doesn't make perfect, it makes permanent." That doesn't just go for world-class musicians. It's for mentors and mentees everywhere.

In our Step 2 chapters so far, we've seen how observing your mentor and watching how they handle themselves causes a significant impression on you, not just socially and emotionally, but also *physiologically.*

When you observe your mentor performing a task repeatedly, something in your brain changes to imprint the activity. Here's how your brain allows you to "memorize" what your mentor does:

- You observe or participate in an activity with your mentor
- A neuron sends a signal to a receiving cell
- How strong the junction is between the neuron and the receiving cell will determine how well you will remember the behavior
- *The more you watch, the more the synapse becomes strong, like a well-exercised muscle*

Science tells us that the more you practice or think about a piece of information stored in your brain, the more that particular junction or synapse is going to be used. As the synapse is used more frequently, it grows in strength. This allows the memory to be more vivid and clear in your mind.[50]
So how does that relate to the mentoring relationship?

Observe and engage with your mentor often!

That will reap great benefits for you. It will come in handy if you decide you want to imitate their behavior, especially if it's in the future when the mentor is not physically present.
Here are several key ways to take those synapses to the mental gym and make them stronger:

- Pay attention (focus and concentration)
- Repetition (watch or do the activity often)
- Use more than one sense (hearing + seeing + doing)
- Teach it to someone else

Ashley, a director in a law firm that specializes in environmental litigation, took those guidelines to heart. She wanted to memorize the success of her peer mentor, Jack, so that she could do what he had modeled in her future business dealings. She shared the following about her experience:

"Jack is the best negotiator I know. He is a friendly, self-effacing guy with a smile as wide as Main Street. He's the first to make a joke on himself, like 'I spent $40 dollars on this haircut, do you think I got my money's worth?' Others would laugh as they looked up at his shiny, bald head. He has that lovable country-cousin quality, but he is smart as a whip and our craftiest opponents didn't relish seeing him across the negotiating table. They knew they'd met their match.

"Every chance I could, I would watch Jack do his thing as he sat at the negotiating table, or in any argument or discussion, and see him build bridges to the other side.

"*I paid attention.* I listened to him describe the opponent's likely position. I listened as he rebutted an argument and watched its impact on the other party. I took copious notes. He was like the Zen Master of contracts. I hung on his words.

"*I repeatedly watched him.* Whenever I had an opportunity to shadow him in a negotiation, I took it. Every time I had a chance to listen to his debrief of the deal, I was there.

"*I used several senses to learn from him.* I watched him at the negotiating table, I heard him present to the executive legal team on negotiation status. I helped out by discussing the pros and cons of our arguments with him. I engaged with him.

"*I taught others.* I invited Jack to talk to my work group about creating win-win solutions. Together, we led a lively discussion on how to honor your opponent and craft successful negotiation strategy."

Ashley had taken these guidelines to heart because she wanted to be able to replicate Jack's behaviors when he wasn't present.

She finished with, "I won't forget his model in the art of successful negotiating. How could I? I had strengthened the how-Jack-does-it synapses in my brain."

Practice by observing and engaging with your mentor. Your brain neurons will do their part and ensure that, "Practice doesn't make perfect, it makes permanent."

Questions to Motivate MentorShift

1. What's the most difficult thing that you've memorized?

2. What strategies did you use to successfully make it permanent?

3. Why is it important to repeatedly watch and interact with your mentor?

CHAPTER 36

The Power of Engagement—
Mentees, Roll up your Sleeves

*"Life is not a spectator sport. If you're going to spend your
whole life in the grandstand just watching what goes
on, in my opinion you're wasting your life."*
— JACKIE ROBINSON, BASEBALL HALL OF FAMER

HAVE YOU EVER PLAYED SPORTS and had to sit on the bench for a
while?

It's maddening! Watch the body language of those on the bench in
the big game. Straining forward, moving their bodies with each play,
looking anxiously over to catch the coach's eye—everything about them
says, "Come on! Put me in!"

Nobody wants to only be a spectator. (There might be a few couch
potatoes and armchair adventurers out there...but I think we can agree
that is not the best goal!)

Observing is important, to be sure. From the previous Step 2 chapters,
you know that:

- you need to *observe* your mentor
- your mentor's *example* is powerful
- you will *imitate* desirable actions and attitudes of your mentor
- you will *remember* your mentor's example by repeated exposure

But if you stopped there, you'd be relegated to the bleachers with a
sack of stale popcorn and a no-fizz soda.

You'd be bored to tears and sitting on the bench.

Step 2 says "I Do, You *Contribute*" for an important reason. It moves the mentee from spectator to actor, accomplice and ally.

Plato was the first person in recorded history to say, "We learn by doing." A whole range of other people have said it, done it and taught it since then.

The late Dr. Howard Hendricks, in his book, *Teaching to Change Lives*, wrote:

> "There is a direct correlation between learning and doing. *The higher the learner's involvement, the greater his potential for learning. [emphasis added]* The best learners are participators; they are not merely watching the action from the outside, but are deeply engrossed in it, involved to the hilt. They're also enjoying it more than learners who aren't involved."[51]

Those are impressive outcomes—satisfied learners, fully involved, enjoying it more.

How does this involvement begin?

Collaboration between the mentor and mentee exists all throughout their relationship. Throughout Step 2, you will work together to create opportunities for the mentee to both observe and be involved. In Step 2, you will experience these things:

- Mentor and mentee plan events and activities for the mentee to observe
- Mentor demonstrates job or skill as the mentee observes
- Mentor explains how and why as they go along
- Mentee asks questions during time with the mentor
- Mentee contributes to the activity to strengthen learning

I share a personal illustration here because it clearly illustrates a mentor that knew how to get her mentee involved.

In Chapter 1, I shared that I had been recruited to lead the business planning effort for the multi-billion dollar VentureStar program. You will recall that the to-be-developed reusable commercial space plane had garnered significant attention and interest from the highest echelons of NASA and Capitol Hill. From the moment I stepped foot into my first meeting on the project, I received endless invitations (aka command performances) to present program progress to high-ranking government and industry leaders.

With much of this responsibility new to me, I needed a mentor.

Christine was the president of one of our divisions. She had an impressive career in domestic and international finance and banking. (Step 1 – I Do.) The VentureStar project was getting so much attention that the CFO of my corporation had requested that she mentor me. Lucky for me!

Over the course of a year, she led me through her intuitive version of the four steps. With her credentials, she clearly satisfied Step 1 qualifications. Here is how she led me through Step 2.

Mentor and mentee plan events and activities for the mentee to observe

Christine practiced Share by Showing mentoring. She and I planned opportunities where I could go with her and observe her in action. We planned together that I would:

- Visit her company headquarters
- Meet her staff and employees
- Listen in on several of her staff meetings
- Watch her present at high-level meetings

Mentor demonstrates job or skill as the mentee observes

One of Christine's primary goals was to groom me to present to executive audiences with executive-level presentations. She invited me to join her as she presented to senior industry and government audiences. I took copious mental notes of how she:

- Prepared, designed, opened and closed the presentation
- Made compelling points
- Integrated data with key message takeaways
- Handled difficult questions or an unreceptive audience
- Dressed professionally and cultivated a personal style

Mentor explains how and why as they go along

We discussed the meeting objectives ahead of time and then debriefed after each event.

She would say, for example, "I plan to recommend that we don't use bank financing until several years after project start. I'm doing this because the lending institutions will want to see industry-sponsored equity commitment to the project first, as well as some locked-down contracts in place."

She was deliberate to include not just the how but the why of her decisions.

Mentee asks questions throughout time with the mentor

I was overflowing with questions.

- Why did she choose that set of data points?
- Why did she opt to address that question in a later session?
- How could she keep her calm when that audience member was attacking her recommendation?

Again, her faithfulness to debrief allowed me greater insight into how and why she acted as she did.

Mentee contributes to the activity to strengthen learning

We also planned where I would contribute so that I could be involved in the process. I would...

- Study and help prepare the executive-level presentation packages
- Present some portions of the overall presentation when appropriate
- Take part in round-table discussions offering my point of view and knowledge base

I was learning more than just tactical skills when I was with her. I was keenly watching the presence she had with executives and clients and how she handled her employees. I essentially shadowed her in whatever she was doing at her office or when we were out in the field.

When mentees are invited to contribute in this way, they are *immersed* in the learning process—and the learning sticks.

Nicole had a college roommate, Jen, who studied abroad in Argentina. Although she had been working towards a Spanish minor for three years, she returned from her trip speaking better Spanish after just four months. Her house hosts mentored her through Spanish using their own version of the "I Do, You Contribute" model. Imagine those dinner table conversations! When Nicole ran into her at their 10-year reunion, she observed that Jen was still pretty impressive as she chatted with her former Spanish teacher—in Spanish. Learning through immersion is significantly more effective than trying to study a topic and retain the information.

And guess what? Neuroscientists agree. A 2012 study shows that students who learned by being immersed in a new topic were better at comprehending *and* retaining the information compared to their peers who were not fully immersed.[52] This is the exact reason that Jen's Spanish developed so rapidly and stayed with her.

Mentee, you can see how a Share by Showing approach keeps you involved and contributing? From Day One, you won't be sitting in the bleachers or on the bench.

Humorist Will Rogers punched home Step 2 when he said, "Even though you are on the right track you will get run over if you just sit there."

Mentees, don't sit there—roll up your sleeves and get engaged!

 Questions to Motivate MentorShift

1. When you are learning something new, how does it feel to sit the bench? Give an example from your experience.

2. How could you invite your mentee to contribute to the learning process?

3. How would you like your mentor to involve you in the learning process?

CHAPTER 37

The Power of Creative Intention— Purposeful Mentoring so Miles Don't Matter

"Every once in a while, people need to be in the presence of things that are really far away."

— IAN FRAZIER, WRITER AND HUMORIST

PEEK OUT FROM BEHIND a rock a few thousand years ago and you can overhear two cavemen discussing the merits of the latest prehistoric technology.

Stoner: Uga, ugh! Mudge. Look this.

Mudge: Stoner make new rock?

Stoner: Big and round. Push hard. Roll down hill. Stoner smart.

Mudge: Stoner smart. Trog more smart.

Stoner: Trog dumb Neanderthal! How Trog more smart?

Mudge: Trog comes.

    (Enter Trog, Stone Age Chief Knowledge Officer [CKO])

Trog: I'm smarter because I have taken your simplistic rock wheel idea, added a hard carbon steel protective covering, axles and a firepower starter. Imagine this, guys. In thousands of years, cavemen won't need to roll a round rock wheel down a hill for speed. Maybe they just ignite firepower (remember, we already discovered that—think synergy!) through an engine box and the wheels carry the chassis anywhere it wants to go. Imagine the future! You guys are thinking like low-foreheaded knuckle-draggers!

Stoner: Oog. (Scratches head.) Trog smarter.

Mudge: (Grunt.) Second that.

How fast things change! Trog, the Stone Age futurist with his forward-thinking ideas, left his caveman peers spinning their rocky wheels.

Twenty-first century futurist, Bill Gates, prophetically said, "This is a fantastic time to be entering the business world, because business is going to change more in the next 10 years than it has in the last 50."[53]

You've witnessed that and been part of it! In a nanosecond, new game-changing ideas are spawned and the future is never the same. You know that unless you continually read, think and change, you will be left rolling the stone ball downhill.

Mentoring must look to the future too. The face of mentoring has transformed in the past few years.

Thirty years ago, a common mentoring model looked like this:

- Mentor was much older than mentee (senior exec mentoring early/mid-career employee)
- Always face-to-face
- Advice oriented; a clear giver and receiver.
- Mentoring hopes led to promotions up the ladder—which could mean a lifelong career with one company

Today, a few things have changed, or perhaps I should say, exploded exponentially. Internet. Social Media. Networks.

Now a mentoring model can often look like this:

- Virtual/Global
- Community-oriented
- Peer-to-peer
- "Upside down" mentoring—younger to older employees
- Learning chat rooms/exchanges
- File/document/idea sharing
- Minimal face-to-face time

Dynamic learning networks, such as the River software product by Triple Creek Associates, allows an employee to connect with multiple, competency-matched learners and advisors, mine data or receive answers to questions across a geographically unlimited space and collaborate in a learning community—all in real-time.

Trog, our Stone Age CKO, would be impressed.

At this point, you might be asking, "How do MentorShift principles fit in with today's highly technical, far-flung workplace?"

- Can concepts like 'with-mentoring' and Share by Showing dovetail with the dynamic, modern learning systems of today?
- Can "Step 2 – I Do, You Contribute" actually work when my mentee is a thousand miles away?"

The answer is a resounding 'yes' and it calls for creative intention.

As you've seen so far, MentorShift principles go like this:

- When you mentor, be the real deal
- When you mentor, take your mentees with you when possible; they need to observe you and contribute to the task for greatest learning
- When you mentor, Share by Showing; move around, get away from the conference table and out into your world

To the wired-in, fully connected individual, I offer these ideas to help you integrate technology and distance with MentorShift principles:

MentorShift *Ideas:*

- Even if you have an online community of hundreds of other learners and advisors via mentoring software, you still sit next to someone at your work setting. If you mostly telework, you still meet up with others face-to-face for meetings occasionally. That is when you can Share by Showing.

- Are you a tech-savvy employee? Sit down *with* your colleagues who may not feel comfortable and show them how to get dialed in to the learning network. Teach them how to get data and make online connections faster.

- If you want to observe a mentor giving a presentation and you live in Cincinnati and she lives in Orlando, hook in live through a webcast or ask her to video it. You need to see her in action, be with her virtually, then you can debrief. There are plenty of ways to record the activity so you pick up the content and the intangibles.

  If a webinar or video opportunity is not possible, at a minimum, you can debrief with her afterwards to gain from her experience.

The bottom line is that today, you have to be creative and purposeful when mentoring over the miles. You don't live in the 19th century where the blacksmith was teaching his apprentice how to make horseshoes while they lived together and worked side-by-side every day.

Nor do you want to be there! More and more, you stretch across continents to connect. You need to jump in and mentor with all that advancing technology has to offer.

Now here's a caveat.

I would be remiss in our discussion of leveraging technology to mentor if I didn't share a concern. I worry that as you strive to excel at distance-mentoring and embrace the benefits of dynamic learning solutions, you might be tempted to stray from timeless MentorShift principles.

I urge you to use technology to mentor across the miles…and I urge you never to forget the human element of mentoring.

It's a fine balance.

If you use mentoring software that allows you to be mentored by many others you likely will never meet, you may get every single piece of data on how to build a needed electrical part online. You may watch many webcasts that build your understanding of the design process. And, if for some reason the design fails, you can get corrective action, failure analysis and encouragement from your online network.

This solves your immediate problem, task or assignment.

And yet, the human element of connection is missing. The mentor. The teacher.

What about the wisdom shared over a cup of coffee?

What about learning the intangibles, such as empathy, self-control and knowing when to speak up at the right time?

What about the pat on the back (a real one) and an "atta boy or girl" from someone who has taught you something in a tense and trying time?

I recently interviewed Toby, a new college grad who is just hitting his stride in his first job as a health care professional. When I asked him about the role of technology for him as it relates to mentoring, he offered this reply:

> "It's true that technology has become a staple in our personal and professional lives especially in my generation. I often hear my own granddad groaning about text messaging and Facebook taking over everyone's lives! Younger generations are pegged as being obsessed with technology because that is how we've learned to communicate.

> "But here's an important distinction. We have never been mentored through Instagram or Snapchat. We have been raised to use technology for fun, communication, and information gathering, but nobody uses technology as the crux of their mentoring relationships. I think it's still essential to have a strong face-to-face presence for effective mentoring to occur. There's no replacement for that."

Bill Gates famously said, "Technology is just a tool. In terms of getting the kids working together and motivating them, the teacher is the most important."[54]

I quote him because there probably aren't many on the face of the planet more committed to technological advances for learning purposes than Bill Gates.

Yet he elevates the teacher.

I recently saw a rather touching cartoon. A schoolteacher is sitting at her desk listening attentively as a grateful, scruffy-haired student speaks to her.

The caption reads, "Everyone was there to shake my hand when I won the spelling bee, but you were there to hold my hand when I was practicing for the spelling bee."

Mentor creatively through technology, become the smartest "high-foreheaded modern human" you can become (hats off to Trog) and never forget the power of person-to-person mentoring.

Questions to Motivate MentorShift

1. Rate your technology savvy from 1–10 when it comes to social learning networks. How would you like to increase it? What will you do to accomplish that?

2. What are the positive elements of online knowledge sharing and learning? What are the downsides?

3. Do you feel there is difference between knowledge sharing and wisdom sharing? Describe.

Summary
Step 2
SHOW.
– I Do, You Contribute –

- Mentor and mentee plan events and activities for the mentee to observe

- Mentor performs tasks and skills as the mentee observes

- Mentor explains how and why as they go along

- Mentee asks questions throughout time with the mentor

- Mentee contributes to the activity to strengthen learning

GROW.

"It takes courage to grow up and become who you really are."
— E. E. Cummings, American poet

Step 3
GROW.
– You Do, I Contribute –
Characteristics

- Mentor challenges mentee to take the lead responsibility

- Mentor equips mentee with success-oriented methodologies

- Mentee performs the task, putting into practice what the mentee has taught

- Mentor observes, helps when needed, offers support

- Mentor provides evaluation through frequent feedback

- Mentor offers correction when necessary

- Mentor encourages by highlighting strengths and successes

CHAPTER 38

Just Do It—
Make the Most of Your Yearning,
Churning, Burning for Learning

*"For the things we have to learn before we can
do them, we learn by doing them."*

— ARISTOTLE

NOW I'M NOT A FOURTH CENTURY BC world-renown philosopher, but doesn't Aristotle's quote above seem a little counter-intuitive at first blush?

"For the things we have to learn before we can do them, we learn by doing them."

After pondering that awhile, I can see it in a hundred ways. I'm sure you can think of a few things that you wouldn't know if you hadn't actually done them.

Let's think about eating sushi. You can eagerly read about it in *Sushi for Dummies*. Your friend can say, "Oh, the squid at Sushi Den is out of this world!" You can sit next to your colleague at the neighborhood sushi bar and watch him devour an eight-piece Caterpillar Roll and see his eyes roll back in unspeakable delight.

But until you take the action to place one of the squeaky, slimy little devils onto your palate, replete with a snap of ginger and some tongue-burning wasabi, you don't really *know* sushi.

You learn by doing

Let's make the necessary and welcome leap from raw fish to learning through mentoring.

A kindergarten poster succinctly displayed: "Learning is 5% hearing, 10% seeing, and 85% doing." I don't know that those are proven statistics but the sentiment rings true.

Mentee, you can watch your mentor all day long, admire their example and vow to imitate it, but until you *do something,* you are not experiencing learning to its fullest degree.

In Step 3, the mentee steps into the lead position. The mentor is there to support, encourage and contribute where needed. But the mentee is far-and-away the doer.

You learn by doing.

Institutions of higher learning know this well. At MIT Sloan, they have built a students' Action Learning Lab whereby the students engage in action learning experiences around the world.

- Student teams work with their Host Companies on four-month project engagements designed to tackle real-world problems.

- In late September, faculty members match the best-qualified teams to their preferred Host Companies.

- From October through December, the teams work on campus with their Host Companies, building their client relationships through online collaboration and weekly conference calls. Teams conduct research, interviews, and analysis that will be critical for their future work in the field.

- In January, teams work on-site full-time at their Host Companies' offices for at least three weeks.[55]

Students blog about their work in a coffee company in Thailand, an electrical vehicle company in Malaysia, a health company in Argentina, among many others.

These students are busy *doing!*

Although your business may not offer international action learning experiences, opportunities exist everyday to learn by doing things you have observed from your mentor's example.

You learn by teaching someone else

Years ago I attended Dr. Stephen Covey's "Seven Habits of Highly Effective People" seminar. Dr. Covey and his staff repeatedly asked us to teach what we had learned during the class sessions to someone back at our workplace within the next day or two.

Why do this?

Dr. Covey posed a challenging question: "If you had known you would be teaching this material to someone else within 48 hours, would it have made a difference in your learning experience?"

I had to admit to myself that I might have listened up a little better if I had anticipated teaching it to someone else.

I decided to put it to the test by teaching what I'd learned and doing it quickly. I took my new seminar knowledge back to my workplace. I approached my colleague and ventured, "Hey, Malik, can I teach you what I just learned in my class?"

Fortunately, Malik was willing to set aside some time and listen as I walked him through the material. He asked a few questions that caused me to reflect more on the material and even go back and re-read my notes. It didn't take long to understand the genius of Dr. Covey's suggestion—I grew when I passed on what I'd learned.

When we teach someone else what we have learned, *we learn twice*: Once when we receive, and again when we give. Receiving begins the learning process; teaching someone else completes it.[56]

You are rewarded for learning by doing

My colleague, Randy Wilhelm, is the CEO of Knovation, a company that creates innovative, personalized learning solutions that brings learning alive for kids. He coined a term for that special moment of discovery that adults and kids everywhere have experienced when they learn how to do something new for the first time.

He calls it the "warmth of knowing."

Randy portrays it this way: "When you discover something for the first time, when you do it and all the pieces come together, when you have that

'Aha!' moment and the lights go on, I believe there's a visceral response—a warmth inside that rewards you for knowing something new.

"That feeling says, 'Wow, I'm *excited* that I learned something new.' But it goes deeper than that. It also means you're getting closer to discovering your meaning as a human being. People have a natural curiosity—a desire to know. We are innately, completely and unconditionally wired that way."

Think about it. What was the last thing you did that you really hadn't done before? Did it puff your chest up just a little bit more when you experienced that "warmth of learning?"

You felt proud, gratified, self-satisfied.

You are wired to learn by doing. Mentoring relationships satisfy this ever-present yearning for learning because mentor and mentee are both teachers and learners at the same time.

Pablo Picasso, one of the most influential artists of the 20th century offered, "I am always doing that which I cannot do, in order that I may learn how to do it."

Step 3 says Just Do It.

 ## Questions to Motivate MentorShift

1. Is it difficult to move from learning by listening and watching to learning by doing? Why or why not?

2. Do you consider yourself a lifelong learner? What's something new you've learned in the past month? Week?

3. Which of your five senses do you use when you learn by doing? Why is this important?

CHAPTER 39

Learning is Not Just a Spectator Sport— So Start Playing!

"Do you know what my favorite part of the game is? The opportunity to play."
— MIKE SINGLETARY—FORMER CHICAGO BEARS LINEBACKER, NFL COACH

"OKAY, LORI, SO YOU'RE as ready as you'll ever be," Christine said with an encouraging but weary smile.

I looked around the hotel suite, littered with papers, laptops, and crushed paper coffee cups. I surveyed the worn-out faces of our team. All five of us had that glazed-over look that comes with finishing up a project at two in the morning, knowing that D-Day is in six hours.

Have you been there before? Those are days and nights of intense preparation, last-minute data coming in as you finish your pitch charts, a possible computer meltdown and a couple of runs to the nearby print shop.

Whew. We would make it to the meeting, adding new meaning to the saying, "Hot off the press."

Mentor challenges the mentee to take the lead responsibility

Six hours later, I was suited up and ready for my presentation to the top brass of our company. It was my first shot out of the barrel to reveal the status of our business plan and progress against our milestones.

Christine's parting words as she had left the hotel suite were, "Okay, over to you. You can do this and I'll be there with you. I'll jump in if you get in a really tough spot."

Mentor equips mentee with success-oriented methodologies

Christine and I had done a practice run on the presentation several times. She had fired the questions at me as if she were my company's CEO.

- Why do you think we can capture that market share?
- How will we meet those delivery milestones?
- What are your recommendations for the dividend policy?

Sometimes those preparatory sessions were referred to as the murder board, for good reason.

She also counseled me on my presence. She reminded me, "Remember how I didn't get rattled when you watched me present to the last corporate audience? It's important to maintain your composure. If you don't know the answer, look to one of our team for support or offer to come back with the answer."

In my subconscious I was reliving my golf lessons. Do you know that feeling of standing at the tee, trying to remember so many things that you shoot the worst hook or slice you've ever seen?

Don't think about the swing. Just do it. It's all in there somewhere. And I knew she had my back.

When we finished the practice run, I was ready.

Mentee performs the task, putting into practice what the mentor has taught

Dressed in my gray pinstripe, serious suit, I strode confidently to the front of the room at 8 a.m. sharp—laser pointer in hand, sweaty palms out of sight. I delivered my opening salvo and began sailing through my introduction.

"Stop right there," our CFO directed.

I'd only made it through the title slide and half of the next one.

The dam broke and the flood of questions began rolling in. Some went as we'd rehearsed; a couple I'd not even contemplated. I guess that's why my audience ran a multi-billion-dollar corporation: They knew how to ask the important questions.

When our CFO drilled down mercilessly into our financing plan, my sweaty palms became the least of my worries. Now it was survival, because this man could spar with the savviest bankers on Wall Street.

Mentor observes, helps when needed, offers support

Before my desperate eyes could beg help from Christine, she stepped in.

"Oh yes, Jim," she confidently said. "We anticipated that potential roadblock. We plan to mitigate the risk by entry-point investments from Company X and Y. X has already signed a memorandum of understanding and Y is at least at the table."

Our CFO nodded and said, "Great, I didn't know we'd identified those early investors. Go ahead with the next slide, Lori."

Two hours later, the meeting was finished. As I learned by leading the presentation, I had been stretched in confidence and experience that morning.

Mentee, learning by leading is one of the most effective ways for you to develop. It allows you to take risks, mitigate issues, and adjust behaviors—all with your mentor serving as a life preserver if needed.

A recent study examined up-and-coming leaders in the IT world and let them run their own enterprise-wide project. Upon completion, 76% of participants said that learning by leading was the most effective training they experienced.[57]

Mentor—will you commit to provide your mentee with leadership opportunities? Mentee—will you ask for those chances to step up?

 Questions to Motivate MentorShift

1. What is rewarding about when your mentor hands over the baton to you? What is challenging?

2. As a mentor, how much should you help when needed? In what circumstances?

3. Mentee, how do you know when you are ready to step up and take the lead in Step 3 – You Do, I Contribute?

CHAPTER 40

Brief Debriefs—
Faithful, Frequent Feedback

"Feedback is the breakfast of champions."
— KEN BLANCHARD, MANAGEMENT EXPERT

CHRISTINE AND I WERE talking over a cup of coffee a few hours after I'd completed the presentation. "So...how did I do, Christine? I mean, *really,* how do you think it went?"

Mentor provides evaluation through frequent feedback

Christine replied, "Good start, Lori, you can be proud of the preparation and presentation you delivered today. And, it's clear we have a boatload of work ahead of us. Are you feeling like you need a nap?"

We both laughed, recalling the 2 a.m. scramble to get there and feeling relieved that it was behind us. Now we could assess our leaders' responses to what I'd proposed.

Christine and I conducted a comprehensive debrief. She offered comments on my delivery, audience reactions, how I'd facilitated the discussion and where I needed to refocus and redirect.

Mentor offers correction when necessary

At one point I asked, "How should I take Jim's comment that in some areas I only had 'a plan for a plan?'"

"He was pushing hard on you on that point, Lori. Our leadership wants to see more rigorous milestones and the steps to achieve them. For instance, you said, 'We plan to have our manufacturing prospective schedules complete in three months.' Jim was surely thinking, 'Where are those plans *right now?*'"

"But, there are so many moving pieces!" I swiftly defended. "The engineers are still working major design elements and we can't plan the factory schedule when the engineering is still in flux."

"You're expected to be on top of that. You need to be meeting with the engineering design team to influence that process, not use it as an excuse."

I considered that, evaluating the enormity of the task to keep the engineering and factory teams in sync.

Christine continued, "I have one more coaching item for you. You are a fairly young female, presenting to an audience of mostly older, much more experienced men. That can be a tough assignment. You always need to ask yourself, 'How do I want to be perceived by this audience?'

"As women, we need to really attend to our delivery style. When John asked you if you'd signed up the investment banking visits, you were a little embarrassed because you hadn't yet done it, so you made light of it. You are funny and might use your humor to brush over a mistake. You can be collegial but show that you are very serious about what you are doing."

(Are we finished with this debrief yet? I wondered.)

Mentor encourages by highlighting strengths and successes

"So, do you have any questions for me about these observations?" Christine asked.

"Okay, I've got it, Christine. Thanks once again for all your input and support—although some of it is not easy to hear."

"Lori, you have signed up to lead an incredibly tough undertaking. Today you entered the lion's den for the first time and did well. Your chart deck was organized and you had analyzed what your audience's key biases would be ahead of time. I believe Jim and the other leaders left the meeting feeling like this was a good first step. And, as I said, there is a lot of hard work ahead."

Okay, then, I thought, this was a lot to chew on. Words can't describe how much I valued her open, balanced and honest comments.

Mentors, you can see that Christine's feedback model had the necessary elements for success. These practices are key ones for you to follow as you debrief with your mentees.

- *Consistent* – this was her practice. While she mentored me, we regularly debriefed about my presentations and project leadership.
- *Specific* – feedback was issue-focused and information-rich—never critical. She was clear on who, what, when and where in her examples.
- *Direct* – she was clear and straightforward. She spoke to me face-to-face thus reducing opportunity for misunderstanding through an e-mail or text.
- *Open* – she invited my questions and reflections on the feedback.
- *Expressed appreciation* – she always ended our feedback sessions with encouragement about future goals and performance.

Dr. Timothy C. Daughtry and Dr. Gary R. Casselman compare criticism with feedback by saying, "Criticism is driven by the frustration and fears of the giver, not from the needs of the recipient...In contrast, feedback has an air of caring concern, respect, and support. Far from being a sugar cookie, feedback is an honest, clear, adult-to-adult exchange about specific behaviors and the effects of those behaviors."[58]

Christine did a great job of balancing the good, bad and a little bit of the ugly.

It's that "bad and ugly" part that mentors often find difficult to express and mentees find hard to accept.

It's worth a closer look so you can appreciate the kindness of correction.

 Questions to Motivate MentorShift

1. Why is it important to consistently debrief in Step 3? What does it do for the mentee? The mentor?

2. What is some feedback you have received from your mentor that has genuinely helped you?

3. What is some feedback you've given your mentee that was a bit difficult for you to give? Why?

CHAPTER 41

Kind Correcting—
Sometimes You Have to Hurt to Help

"A coach is someone who can give correction without causing resentment."
— John Wooden, Basketball Hall of Famer and coach

Have you heard the proverb, "Better are the wounds of a friend than the kisses of an enemy?"

At the core, I don't think any of us really relish the thought of being corrected even by a mentor or friend.

Remember how in Christine's feedback to me, midway through, I jumped in and practically shouted, "But there are so many moving parts!" That was my way of saying, "No more! I don't want to hear what I might need to improve! I only want to know where I've done well!"

Like me, you've been corrected at times. You might not have asked for it…and even if you were open to it, you probably didn't like it. But you are smart enough to know that sometimes you have to hurt to help.

In my career and personal life, I've delivered countless presentations to all types of audiences and led numerous projects. I've received both praise and correction. Two instances of correction stand out in my mind, one mine and one a colleague's, and serve as a lesson to me again and again.

In the first, I had been presenting our project's quarterly updates to the CEOs of half a dozen major corporations throughout that year. I would stand at the front of the room and look out and think, "Wow, these CEOs represent 40-billion-dollars worth of annual revenues." It was an honor to be standing up front.

The day after one quarterly CEO meeting, as we sat at his office table, my boss and mentor, Jerry, began, "So, Lori, you won't be presenting at the next CEO meeting. Though you had all the investment banking data down pat, you took too long to get to your core message. When you have these individuals' attention, you have to treat it like pure gold."

I stared blankly at him, feeling a little sick as I digested the news.

"These C-level execs have limited time to give you. You need to respect that and give them the direct, important message right off the bat. You kept them waiting too long for the meat of the matter."

I cringed. I felt like the cartoon vaudeville character that was dancing and singing gaily on stage only to catch a sideways glimpse of the hook—the dreaded hook—coming from the side stage to yank her into the curtains.

Jerry was not unkind, but he was firm in his comments. He understood that I would feel hurt by this news. Nevertheless, he had to correct my behavior.

"But, can't I have one more opportunity to fix it? C'mon Jerry, one more shot," I entreated him.

"Not at the next meeting. I'm going to give Marty the stage next time. You will have other opportunities. Remember the message about respecting your audience's time and what they've come for. Treat it like gold."

Later, when I considered that the Warren Buffetts of the world have their messages delivered to them in sound bites and calendars scheduled for them in five-minute increments, I understood why Jerry had corrected me as he did.

I will never forget how his words hurt to help. They shaped me as a speaker today; that's the lasting impact of a kind correction. Whenever I present now, no matter the audience: A seventh-grade class, a roomful of C-level executives, moms and dads at the PTA meeting, I have been transformed in my attitude and approach.

I realize that I have been given a gift of an audience's time and attention; I seek to honor that by delivering a forthright presentation that meets their needs directly and exceeds their expectations.

I still thank Jerry today for his kind correction.

Despite his best intentions, however, a mentor giving feedback in Step 3 can make a mistake once in awhile.

Josh, a promising analyst in a small Internet start-up company, shared such an experience with me.

"My mentor, Darrah, had observed my efforts on a project over several months. I admired her work as a leader and diligently took to heart the gems she passed on to me. I was looking forward to receiving her feedback about how she felt I was performing on the project.

"After a few exchanges, Darrah began sharing where I could improve. She cited where I'd failed to get the team coordinated on one deliverable, where my team had missed a milestone to our client, how I'd hired a less-than-effective employee. It seemed like her criticisms were lasting an eternity."

I could see the anguish pass across Josh's face as he continued, "I could feel myself tensing up. I was thinking, 'When is she going to get to the part that I did right?' After all, we were about ready to take the project over the finish line.

"When she saw that I was feeling defensive, she expressed that she thought I had oceans of potential and then went on to share a couple of things I'd done well.

"By then, I wasn't even in 'receive mode'—I just wanted to make my exit. I left that day feeling like I never wanted to lead a project again."

Josh paused and his demeanor relaxed.

"Some time later, Darrah came to me and said, 'Josh, I've been think-ing about something. Will you please accept an apology from me? I won't ever give feedback again the way I did with you last time we met. Because I recognize the strength you have as a leader, I just so wanted to fix the things I felt you could improve on this particular project—now! I should have balanced my feedback to you, because the last thing I wanted to do was break your spirit. You have your team's respect and are an effective leader to them. I should never have come off the way I did.'"

Josh smiled and concluded, "That comment, in and of itself, proved to me her strength as a mentor. She had laid it on heavily and I'd felt discouraged. She saw her error, acknowledged it, apologized and altered her course of behavior going forward."

Mentor, if you have made Darrah's error and overcorrected, you can follow her example:

- *Acknowledge* your error
- *Apologize* sincerely
- *Adjust* your correction style next time
- *Applaud* and encourage

She handled the overcorrection with humility and grace, reaffirming she is a class-act mentor.

With my mentor, Jerry, and Josh's mentor, Darrah, their words came across as the proverb says—the wounds of a friend. In both cases, he and I clearly needed to hear and learn from them.

Mentors, I have one final note on correction and it's possibly the most powerful way to effectively and positively offer correction to your mentee. (Note: mentees, take this in, because sometimes mentors need correction too!)

Have you heard yourself say to your mentee, "You did a good job preparing for your project *but* you didn't follow through as well as you might have on the execution?"

What part of that statement do you think your mentee heard and remembered?

Probably not much more than, "You didn't follow through well on the execution."

The troublesome word "but" is the derailer. *That word steals the goodwill you intended with "You did a good job preparing for your project."*

Mentor—when offering corrective feedback, do your best to use the word "AND" and not "BUT." It won't come naturally at first, but you can work at it.

You can say, "You did a good job preparing for your presentation AND you didn't follow through as well as you might have on the execution."

Both are true. Both need to be heard by your mentee.

Mentee—welcome the helpful words from your mentor. If your mentor is a ForMentor, they are truly giving you some counsel to benefit you.

It's true, as author L.M. Heroux so aptly expressed, that we can all use some "direction correction!"

 Questions to Motivate MentorShift

1. When is a time that you've received correction and it truly helped you?

2. What's difficult about offering correction? Receiving it?

3. Think of a correction you would like to give to someone. Practice using AND between the affirmation and the correction.

Summary
Step 3
GROW.
– You Do, I Contribute –

- Mentor challenges mentee to take the lead responsibility

- Mentor equips mentee with success-oriented methodologies

- Mentee performs the task, putting into practice what the mentor has taught

- Mentor observes, helps when needed, offers support

- Mentor provides evaluation through frequent feedback

- Mentor offers correction when necessary

- Mentor encourages by highlighting strengths and successes

SECTION 6

GO.

"You're off to Great Places!
Today is your day!
Your mountain is waiting,
So... get on your way!"

— Dr. Seuss, from his book, *Oh, the Places You'll Go!*

GO.
Step 4
– You Do –
Characteristics

- Mentee performs skill without mentor being present

- Mentee continues to build in knowledge, expertise and maturity

- Mentor is available for consultation when needed

CHAPTER 42

Liftoff!—
The Mentee Launches

*"The excitement really didn't start to build until the trailer—
which was carrying me, with a space suit with ventilation
and all that sort of stuff—pulled up to the launch pad."*
— ALAN SHEPARD, JR., FIRST AMERICAN IN SPACE;
WALKED ON THE MOON, 1971

"FIVE, FOUR, THREE, TWO, ONE...it's main engine ignition...pyro...
and liftoff! The Atlas II rocket has cleared the tower carrying the
UHF F7 satellite...engines burning well...all systems nominal...a beautiful
day here at Cape Canaveral Air Force Station."

I sat upright and wide-eyed as I listened to the Voice of Atlas announce
the Atlas II rocket's second-by-second progression upward out of the atmosphere. It was carrying a multimillion-dollar payload into orbit.

Earlier that evening, before countdown, everyone could feel the intense
energy in the Mission Control Center. Each command station—propulsion,
power, attitude control, and the rest—had just given its approval and, in
turn, crisply announced "Go Atlas, Go Centaur," the code for "launch is
ready, good to go."

When the last station had declared its readiness, the ignition fired.

At last—liftoff!

My boss, Ken Mattingly, had invited my team and me to come to the
Mission Control Center and observe this launch. (Ken is a former Apollo
astronaut. You might remember him from the movie *Apollo 13* as the astronaut who didn't go on the ill-fated mission because he'd been exposed to

the measles. Ken proved to be a key player in bringing the astronauts safely back to earth.)

We had worked on this mission and others like it for months. Our engineering and operational teams had executed numerous tests and quality control checks to ensure success. Of course, there's always tension until the payload has successfully separated from the launch vehicle, but that's part of the glory of the achievement.

I won't forget witnessing my first launch. In particular, I won't forget how the rocket was launched at the appropriate time and not a minute before—all systems had to be GO.

That's also true for our mentees—minus the ignition, pyro, and lift-off! But the analogy is strong and clear.

Mentors, by Step 4 – You Do, you have prepped your mentees. They have observed you in action, followed your example, learned by contributing, and even taken the lead.

Now it's time to launch.

Mentee performs skill without mentor being present.

Mentors, when you reach that time when you launch your mentees into their own orbits, like the rocket engineers, you'll want to do it at the right time and not a minute too soon. But how will you know when they're ready?

Watch for these indicators when your mentees:

- Exhibit increased confidence
- Have less need for regular contact
- Take the initiative consistently
- Show interest in developing themselves
- Desire to help others learn
- Feel excited to be on their own

When Richard Sherlock, seasoned pilot for a major commercial airline, had his first solo flight, he showed all the readiness indicators for Step 4.

As a newbie private pilot, Richard received many hours of training from Brent, his highly qualified flight instructor. Brent had taught Richard the fundamentals of flying as they'd logged more than 16 hours of practice flight together. They had done the requisite pre-flight checks, takeoffs and landings, engine stalls and simulator training. Recently, Brent had been giving Richard lead responsibility when sharing the cockpit with him.

One sunny spring afternoon as they sat at the end of the taxiway in the single engine Cessna, Brent said, "Richard, do you know what today is? Today—it's *your* airplane."

Then Brent promptly opened the cockpit door and hopped out.

As Richard later said, "I wasn't 100% confident yet, but since I was first in line for takeoff, I didn't have time to do anything but fly the airplane. It was the weirdest feeling in the world, but I felt great. Brent's words and the procedures were engrained in my mind. I wasn't scared and knew I could handle it. I felt the tension that comes with all good things, but I had confidence in his ability to rate my readiness."

Mentees, can you relate to Richard's story?

Are you ready for launch?

 Questions to Motivate MentorShift

1. Mentor—if you've assessed that your mentee is ready for Step 4, describe the conversation you might have with them to prep them to be on their own.

2. What could be the consequences of moving on too soon? Too late?

3. Mentee, how might you feel when you've launched on your own?

CHAPTER 43

When the Spacecraft Separates, It's a Big Doggone Deal— Your Own Mentoring Mission

"A man with money is nothing compared to a man on a mission."
— DOYLE BRUNSON, POKER HALL OF FAME INDUCTEE

I HATE TO SEE A GROWN man cry or a grown woman for that matter. But I have witnessed it more than once during my days in the space industry.

It's a good thing that 99% of the time, they are tears of joy!

Picture the same Mission Control Center where I'd witnessed the Atlas II rocket launch, this time from the viewpoint of team members who built the satellite payload. Indeed, some of these brilliant, dedicated men and women had worked on this one project for 10, 15, 20 years—practically their entire working lives.

These missions explore the far reaches of the solar system, provide sensitive data to the military or beam back facts affecting the weather in your hometown. Whatever the mission, it is unique, specific, meaningful and a grand accomplishment. You can see why finally succeeding would create a lump in the throat.

Back to Mission Control. After the rocket has launched, it's nail-biting time until it's known that the spacecraft has separated and injects into its proper orbit.

As the satellite and launch team wait for the longed-for confirmation, they hear nothing but the calm, controlled voices of the mission specialists reporting flight status.

"Booster engine cut-off...main engine cut-off..."

And then the good news.

"It's spacecraft separation; the Journey satellite has successfully separated from the second rocket stage and is on its way to explore new horizons..."

The room ERUPTS. What a stirring moment!

Then come the tears of joy. (I know of one project leader who dropped to his knees, clasped his hands to heaven, and shouted, "Thank you, God!")

Needless to say, the team feels fully invested in the mission. When the spacecraft separates, it's a big doggone deal.

Mentee, minus the Mission Control Center theatrics, that scene describes *you!*

Mentee continues to build in knowledge, expertise and maturity

You've succeeded through all the steps. And now, not only can your mentor move to the background of your landscape, you are clearly and intentionally moving forward on your own.

Are you well equipped? As a result of being mentored, have you learned powerful proficiencies? Critical new skills? Fresh passion about your work?

To conclude my story with Christine, our VentureStar project had been progressing for many months. One day she called and said, "I have some news. We have upcoming international projects that require my undivided attention. I'm going to be more of a background supporter to you now. You're good to go now on your own."

Much to my amazement, I confidently said, "Sure. I know you're just a phone call away."

When this time came, I had thought I might feel like Linus without his blanket. But that was far from the case. I genuinely appreciated all she had done *with* me and *for* me. She had been a Share by Showing mentor, consistently reinforcing my learning through Steps 2 and 3. I felt fully ready for Step 4.

I knew her mentoring purpose with me had been accomplished.

Each of our missions in the space industry was indeed unique, specific, and meaningful. So is yours.

When you move on, your mentor may not fall down shouting to the heavens (that could be embarrassing), but you will both know the time is right. You are on your way to exploring new horizons.

The spacecraft has separated.

 Questions to Motivate MentorShift

1. What things begin to change in your mentoring relationship when it's time to separate and be on your own?

2. What would be a consequence of *not* separating?

3. You have a mission that is unique, specific, and meaningful to you. Describe what it is: e.g., a new position, a new way of thinking, a leadership role.

CHAPTER 44

Text, Tweet or Talk—
Your Mentor is Just a Bit or Byte Away

"Be well, do good work and keep in touch."
— GARRISON KEILLOR, STORYTELLER, RADIO HUMORIST

MY FRIEND, ELLIE, related this story about the day her parents visited her for Parents' Day in the late fall of her freshman year at college.

She began, "I had launched out a couple of months earlier and was on my own, traveling down the adventurous road of higher learning. When my parents arrived on campus, I greeted them both with a big hug and welcomed them to my new digs.

"I remember saying, 'Come on, I can't wait to show you where I live and introduce you to some of my new friends. Oh, and Dad, there's this guy I like—you need to meet him.'

"My mom walked into my dorm room, looked bemusedly around my pint-sized space, and her gaze lingered at the burgeoning mess on my bed and floor." Ellie laughed, "Some things are constants in this life! Mom examined me, giving me the quick but comprehensive mom assessment and smiled. I know she was thinking, 'My kid is a happy camper.'

"One month earlier, that had not been the case. I remembered several late-night phone calls home when I was near tears. 'Everything is still so unfamiliar, Mom. When will I really feel settled in?'

"Mom's voice, her encouragement, talking about everything and nothing, was a shelter in the storm of homesickness I was feeling.

"As the counterpoint to my mom's soothing words, Dad would jump on the line with his bright bravado. 'Honey, are you keeping those guys at bay? You tell them what they have to deal with if they get out of line. I arm-wrestled a bear when I was hunting once...you remember that story, don't you?'

"A little bit of peace flooded in with those phone calls. I would hang up and think, 'Okay...I can do this.'

"I had just needed to touch home base.

"Those touch points along the way had given me what I needed to get on my independent way. They were a shot in the arm and the encouragement that everything was going to be all right."

Ellie smiled and said, "By Parents' Day, a team of wild horses could not have dragged me from my cool and happening life as a college student."

Mentor is available for consultation when needed

We all need to touch home base. It might just be the shot in the arm we need.

How wonderful for you as a mentee! You're on your own but your mentor is just a text, tweet or phone call away.

You probably won't be homesick with your voice aquiver like Ellie was, but you will need to touch base occasionally. Here's what it might be like for you:

A quick text: "U should C this team that wrks 4 me. They rock."

A tweet from @launched mentee:

> "Hey Mentor, in less than 140 characters I can tell you that life is good and I got the new job. Can you believe that? Let's get together next time you are in town."

> A phone call: "Hey, call me back when you pick up this voicemail. I have a new project that needs some strategic brainstorming. I'd like to pick your brain a little bit. Thanks, talk to you soon."

You'll want to stay as connected as you need to. Your mentoring relationship is an information-rich, well-cultivated resource for you.

Once I missed an opportunity to reach back to my mentor.

In Chapter 1, I shared my story about changing some priorities so I could take new actions in my life. I chose to transition from a highly visible and exacting project so that I could return to a position with less demand to be away from home.

That was a turning point for me—and it had some consequences. Whereas I had always said "yes" to any job opportunity offered me, now I was beginning to say "no" as I measured the opportunity against other priorities.

I wrestled through some dark nights of the soul as I reconfigured my life and attitudes. I was trading in the Senior VP nameplate dream for something else. There were new and different roads ahead.

These were just the kind of conversations you might like to have with your mentor.

But I didn't call my mentor, Christine.

What was I thinking? For some reason (was it pride?) I worked through those transitions on my own. She had known me well, had witnessed my growth first-hand, and truthfully, had a vested interest in my success.

I ended up immensely fulfilled in my career and happy in my personal life. I have no regrets about the changes I made.

I do recognize this though—*I had foregone a valuable resource by working through these decision points alone.*

Not so today! The great news is that I did reconnect with her eventually and now, many years later, she is still a trusted Friend-tor that I call upon. She still has my back.

As you move on in your career and life and as you mentor others, think of the resource you have who is just a few bits and bytes away.

Remember the winsome space creature, E.T., and his most famous words? He would point his crooked little alien finger at the sky and say, "E.T. phone home."

Mentee—phone home! Your mentor was there to help once. They can be there to help again.

 ## Questions to Motivate MentorShift

1. When might be a time when you would want to connect with your mentor after you have moved to Step 4 – You Do?

2. What's your preferred way to connect? Why?

3. As a mentee, what happens when you try to go it alone?

CHAPTER 45

You May Have More Experience Than You Think— Take a Look at Your Everyday Life

"Experience is a great teacher."
— JOHN LEGEND, GRAMMY AWARD-WINNING
SINGER/SONGWRITER

I've LONG BELIEVED THAT many of us really have been mentoring by doing these four steps throughout our lives and just didn't really have a name for it.

It's happened as fathers have taught their sons to hit a line drive down third base, as mothers have taught their daughters to bake a rocking batch of oatmeal cookies, as shop teachers show their students how to use a lathe or a drill when creating that first model car.

It has happened as bosses help their workers prepare for a presentation, an audit or a sales meeting with a client.

The natural flow of this process happens in everyday ways. It proved true once more to me recently in a humorous way in my own kitchen.

When Martha Stewart quit her television show, *At Home with Martha*, my mother could have just stepped into her apron without missing a beat. Amongst her other immeasurable skills in the culinary domain, Mom has the coolest way of cutting up an onion.

I too have cut up my share of onions in my life. On a good day, my minced was diced, my diced was chopped and my chopped, well, they were small bricks. I always wound up slip-sliding my knife blade all over the cutting board and ended up with teary, burning eyes and a minor laceration or two.

My children would come in the kitchen and just stand and stare as I chopped. They would look at each other and one would ask, "Should an onion really make her that sad? Mom, will you be okay?"

My mother, on the other hand, approaches the bulb with the confidence of an Olympic champion. She holds the onion firmly, cuts it in half and lays it face down. She then cuts a series of lengthwise slices, two vertical slices through the middle and then short chops from one end to the other.

As she holds it, the onion stays together perfectly until the last minute when she releases with flair and voila, it falls on the cutting board in harmoniously cubed pieces.

A domestic goddess in our midst.

Putting aside my foolish pride (after all, I've had a few years in the kitchen too), I asked her to show me her secret.

It was the Four Step MentorShift Process right there at the cutting board.

She is, remember, Martha's clone (Step 1).

She dissected the onion and I stood at the kitchen island studying her every move (Step 2).

I then took the knife and began the process and she offered instruction and corrections here and there (Step 3).

My completed onion was not yet the flawless perfection of hers but I stood a little taller knowing I had gained a new skill. No longer will I have a co-dependent relationship with my food processor, I will take charge at the cutting board and my future onions will reach a new eye-watering height (Step 4).

In a more poignant vein, the fact that we used these Four Steps without recognizing them until later was proven to me through a recent, touching conversation.

After a workshop I'd conducted on "MentorShift—The Four Essential Steps," an older gentleman came up to the podium and waited patiently as I gathered my belongings. I could see that he had something important he wanted to say. When I made it over to where he stood, he shared his story.

"I've had a bit of a revelation today," he began. "I've been doing these four steps and didn't even know it. You see, my 6-year-old grandson recently had a kidney transplant and I've been taking care of him as he recovers. I have the task of giving him nourishment through a feeding tube for each meal. As I have been doing it, his older sister sits with me by his bedside and observes.

"Last week I said to her, 'Honey, you've been watching Grandpa for a few days. Would you like to learn to feed your brother?' Her eyes grew wide and I could tell she felt fearful about taking on something like this by herself.

"'I think so, Grandpa, if you will show me how,' she cautiously said to me. So I took her hands and placed the tubes in them and helped her guide them into the main tube. They fit perfectly and it was the first time she had felt what it was like to connect it. The next day we worked on it again with me guiding her."

He paused as he looked off reflectively as if imagining his grandson with him by his side. Then he continued, "Do you know now who is feeding my grandson? My granddaughter. She has taken over the job, in a hands-on way, of helping her little brother get well."

He finished with a half smile, "See, I was doing these steps and I didn't even know it."

It was gratifying to see this kind man realize that he had passed on such an important skill and, at the same time, grasp the power of this method in connecting his family together.

These four MentorShift steps are in the natural flow of learning even in the most ordinary of life situations.

Your goal is to harness those everyday moments and act them out with intention.

 Questions to Motivate MentorShift

1. When did someone mentor you through the Four Step MentorShift process and you maybe didn't recognize it at the time?

2. Where have you used the Four Step MentorShift process and maybe didn't recognize it at the time?

3. In your current position, in what tasks or skills will you plan to mentor someone else using the Four Step process?

   (Please refer to A-4 "Our Four-Step Roadmap" for a template to get started mapping out the steps together.)

Summary
Step 4
GO.
– You Do –

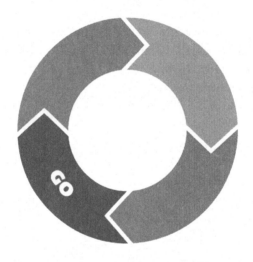

- Mentee performs skill without mentor being present
- Mentee continues to build in knowledge, expertise and maturity
- Mentor is available for consultation when needed

Shifting *Forward*

*For time and the world do not stand still. Change is
the law of life. And those who look only to the past
or the present are certain to miss the future.*

— JOHN F. KENNEDY, JR.

CHAPTER 46

Creating Culture Change— Let's Move a Mountain

"There's nothing wrong with change, if it is in the right direction."
— WINSTON CHURCHILL

IN A RECENT *Forbes* article entitled, "Why Your Employees Are Leaving," the writer begins with this story:

> "One day when I was out getting a coffee, I overheard a man talking on his cellphone. 'We need to be stricter with our hiring practices next year,' he said. 'We want to keep them past a year.' I wanted to turn around and tell him, 'Maybe you don't need to be stricter with your hiring practices. You can bring them in but you're not keeping them. It could be your corporate culture.'"[59]

I read this paragraph and thought, "Aha, that's the ticket! Want to keep employees? Change the corporate culture!"

But that's like doing—what? Climbing Mt. Everest in your pajamas? Kissing your elbow? Achieving world peace by next Saturday?

Several of my senior colleagues and I have tried counting the "culture—changing initiatives" we have seen over the years. Initiatives formed to permeate, infiltrate and agitate our business environs.

We tallied up the times someone from the learning development or communications departments had arrived at our offices armed with a box of how-to books that we were all to read and begin following—or the times that we left an executive staff meeting with the edict to read a new book and pass it down to our troops—always ASAP.

The list of these initiatives was long and varied, some mildly successful, others unfortunately not much more than a puff in the wind.

We concluded that the few initiatives that were quite successful had these things in common:

- Developed on simple principles
- Motivated by an inspirational message
- Sponsored by top leadership
- Driven by middle management
- Executed by all employees
- Carried out over time

These were a respectable set of observations and it was gratifying to see that they dovetail with the credible and compelling description that follows.

Scott Goodson, author of *Uprising: How to Build a Brand – and Change the World – By Sparking Cultural Movements*, shares his wisdom on creating cultural change in a recent *Forbes* article,

> "I've come to believe that the best way to rejuvenate a company culture is to give people inside that company *a fresh idea or driving principle they can embrace, rally around, and act upon.* [emphasis added] It has to be more than words, though—it has to feel more substantial, more engaging, more revolutionary than that. In short: You need to launch a 'movement' within your own company."

That's the cultural change you can expect to see when a company, from CEO to newest hire, embraces the MentorShift process.

Mr. Goodson underscores the movement idea by relating the "Think Different" campaign inspired by Steve Jobs at Apple.

> "We all know the story of Steve Jobs' incredible turnaround at Apple Computer after returning to the company in the late 1990s—it led to a series of amazing product introductions that have continued up to the present. But Apple didn't start with the products—it started with the culture.

"At the time of Jobs' return, the 20-year-old company had lost some sense of its own purpose, its 'specialness.' One of the first things Jobs did was to start a 'Think Different' movement inside the company, particularly aimed at the product developers. Before the outside world ever saw those famous 'Think Different' ads, those two words were appearing on banners and T-shirts at the company's headquarters, ensuring that everyone at the company lived and breathed this philosophy.

"'Steve was inviting everybody in that company to rethink everything,' recalls the longtime Apple ad chief, Lee Clow of TBWA/Chiat/Day. 'At the time, he didn't have any new product yet, and Apple was almost out of business. But to him, the first mission was to get everybody singing off the same song sheet again.'

"By the time 'Think Different' became a public campaign—and an external movement that rallied creative people everywhere around this idea—it was already an established internal movement at Apple.

"It's not easy to spark a movement within a company—it can be a large and ambitious exercise in change management. It may take months (or, to look at it another way, it never ends; transforming a corporate culture tends to be an ongoing process)."[60]

Launching a MentorShift movement in your company
I've seen the MentorShift process revolutionize the way organizations approach mentoring. MentorShift has, in Mr. Goodson's words, *a fresh idea and driving principles you can embrace, rally around, and act upon*. It:

- Challenges and grows every person in the organization regardless of position on the corporate ladder.
- Enlists mentor and mentee to do the full process *together*.
- Transfers skills through consistent Share by Showing activities.
- Multiplies mentoring and carries it forward into the future over time.

By embracing MentorShift principles, you will drive profound culture change in your business.

You can start the movement by deciding to "Think Different." And you can pick up your MentorShift t-shirt in the lobby!

 ## Questions to Motivate MentorShift

1. What successful elements were brought to bear in the "Think Different" movement?

2. When was the last time you were inspired by a culture change you experienced in your company?

3. Does your company culture need a mentoring culture change? Why or why not?

CHAPTER 47

Multiplying the ROI—
When Your Mentee Becomes a Mentor

*"Never doubt that a small group of thoughtful, committed citizens
can change the world. Indeed, it is the only thing that ever has."*

— MARGARET MEAD, CULTURAL ANTHROPOLOGIST

I'VE HEARD IT SAID, "You are not really a mentor until your mentee becomes a mentor."

Do you think that's true?

I'd say, "Of course you are a mentor even if your mentee doesn't develop someone else—and a truly fine one, I'll lay odds—but you aren't yet a multiplying mentor."

And that's where we want to go.

First, let's think about this on the personal front. Have you heard a young couple, married a few years, say, "Our parents are driving us nuts! All they talk about is grandkids. So we bought them a grand-dog. That didn't do it for them."

Why are Granny and Gramps-to-be so intent about their offspring's offspring?

In Chapter 1, "Bravo, Mr. Jobs, We *Can* Put a Ding in the Universe," we thought about an answer to that. We looked at how we are wired to want to leave a legacy, to entrust what we have to the next generation... and the next...and the next.

It's true. Look at Granny's face as she reads *Goodnight Moon* to her young grandson, or Gramps' expression when he teaches his granddaughter how to cast a fly rod.

There's something there that even the best camera could never capture. It's a look that sees the face of the future.

On the business front, a man named Regi Campbell is making a difference as a multiplying mentor.

Regi is a successful entrepreneur who has launched numerous start-up companies, authored books and been recognized as the high technology Entrepreneur of the Year in Georgia.

His striking impact, though, comes through his mentoring outreach. Each year, he mentors a group of eight young up-and-coming executives through a program called Radical Mentoring that he began in 2000.

It is an investment in and out of the workplace, and he is indeed a Share by Showing mentor who spends time with them. He writes:

> "When you mentor younger people, you'll find yourself in all kinds of places. I visit each guy's workplace once during the mentoring year...there are other one-on-one meetings for breakfast or lunch...I've gone to football games, fly-fishing and jet skiing—you name it...Many times in those environments, questions come up, and teachable moments present themselves."[61]

What impresses me about Campbell's example is the multiplier effect of his legacy. Over the past 13 years, he has mentored 100 men. Each man signs a covenant at the beginning of the mentoring year, committing to mentor a group of eight other men at some future point.

If each man held true to his commitment, there would be 800 more men mentored, even if you just stopped there. And if the process continued one step further, there could be up to 6,400 new mentors created.

And what if it doesn't stop there?

You can predict what will happen as a result of this one man's efforts—strong leadership rippling through the workplace for years to come and families shored up through investment in the fathers.

Regi is an equipper. He doesn't let mentoring stop with one individual. Remember our initial definition of mentoring? *He equips them to reproduce the mentoring in someone else.*

In business, we often stop short. I've observed this for many years and it motivated me to write this book.

We may mentor others, but rarely have I seen the spotlight on equipping mentees so that they will become mentors.

This is the attraction of the MentorShift process that you've just walked through. It powerfully develops a mentee so they have a model to develop another person. Recall the MentorShift circle prominently flowing throughout the book? The process is the teacher and, just as the circle, it's meant to be never-ending.

In his book, *Equipping 101*, leadership expert John Maxwell underscores the power of equipping others. With regard to multiplying mentors, he writes:

> "That is my favorite part of the whole process. Once the new leaders do the job well, it becomes their turn to teach others how to do it. As teachers know, the best way to learn something is to teach it. And the beauty of this is it frees me to do other important developmental tasks while others carry on the training."[62]

You're a mentor and through these steps, you've equipped your mentee. So, what's next for you?

 Questions to Motivate MentorShift

1. As a mentee, how do you know when you're fully equipped and ready to move on?

2. Who do you know that is a good equipper? What qualities do they display?

3. Why do you think it's easier to mentor one person and stop there? What would it take for you to become a multiplying mentor?

CHAPTER 48

Move-Mentoring—
The Mentor Moves On and
Mentors Again

"Always in motion is the future."

— Yoda, galactic mentor, from The Empire Strikes Back

I HAVE A COLLEAGUE, Joe, who served as CFO of a multi-billion-dollar company. Joe would refer to those around him who were the wise souls of the organization, those who took the good of the group as their personal mission, as "Yodas."

That was the highest compliment he could pay someone.

He'd say, "Let's get all the Yodas in a room and get their counsel."

It's worth thinking back for a moment to the dear little wrinkly guy.

Yoda was the mentor extraordinaire of the Star Wars series. Besides keeping Luke Skywalker from blasting over to the Dark Side, he also covered a lot of mentoring ground in his hundreds of years of life.

I read that he trained many Jedi younglings—Dooku, Mace Windu, Cin Drallig, Ikrit, Rahm Kota, Tyvokka, Kit Fisto, Ki-Adi-Mundi, Oppo Rancisis, and of course, Luke Skywalker.[63] (Yes, this is the kind of exhaustive research one does as an author.)

At one point or another, anybody who was anybody in the galactic domain had been trained by Yoda.

He was a mentor on the move.

Guess what! That is your goal. You mentor. You move. You mentor well through the Four Steps. You move on to your next mentee.

229

Remember the multiplication principle we just discussed? As you mentor, you are teaching your mentee to mentor also.

I have a strong belief that good mentors, ones who have been bitten by the MentorShift bug, never stop at just one mentee. Have you ever seen someone well known for their care and concern for others say, "That's that. I mentored my one mentee. Check the box. Enough of that."

Jim Rohn, the man many consider the world's foremost business philosopher (as well as author, entrepreneur and motivational speaker), mentored Mark Victor Hansen and Jack Canfield (co-creators, *Chicken Soup* book series) Tony Robbins *(Awaken the Giant Within)* and author-lecturer Brian Tracy *(Eat That Frog)*.

Many mentees.

Poet Maya Angelou, hailed as one of the most renowned and influential voices of our time, mentored Oprah Winfrey as well as the millions of readers who continue to be touched by her books.

A spirit of constant mentoring.

Mentor, keep moving and the movement will multiply.

Or as Yoda would say, "Mentor you will, move on you will."

Questions to Motivate MentorShift

1. Who is a mentor you know that has mentored more than one person? Describe that mentor.

2. Why do you think that mentors who have mentored once will mentor again?

3. Mentor, do you have an idea whom you might mentor next?

CHAPTER 49

Will the Earth Move for You?— The Four-Step MentorShift Process is A Shift that Lasts

*"When an idea reaches critical mass there is no
stopping the shift its presence will induce."*

— MARIANNE WILLIAMSON, NEW YORK TIMES
BESTSELLING AUTHOR

I SAT ON OUR BACK DECK, grabbing a quiet minute after dinner to contemplate the majestic view of Mount Evans framed by the Colorado evening sky. My 81-year-old dad walked out and sat beside me.

"How's the book coming, honey?"

"Oh Dad, it's like my author friend, Mary, told me. 'When you think you are completely done and ready to wrap it up, you're only three rewrites away from really being finished.'"

Dad laughed, "Sometimes I don't even ask you because I don't want to get slugged. I know you've worked on it a long time. Don't worry, you're within spitting distance."

"Spoken like a true cowboy, Dad." I smiled.

My son, Andrew, strode out on the deck, armed with a marshmallow-speared stick and headed for the fire-pit. He said, "Grandpa, are you guys talking about Mom's Four Steps?" Then he grinned and looked at me, "Mom, observe closely how I roast these marshmallows so when you do it you don't burn them to a crisp like you tend to do. Watch my technique now. By the way, which step is that? Two? Three?"

"Watch it buddy, or you'll see what gets burned to a crisp" I said, stoutly defending my marshmallow roasting honor. "And it's step two by the way."

My mom and my daughter, Annie, walked out just then and pulled up chairs to join us. Annie sat down, looked at me pensively and then offered, "Mom, I really didn't mind going with you to your speaking engagement this week. In fact, I actually like helping out even though it's totally embarrassing when you introduce me and make everyone clap for me."

"I love to embarrass you honey, you're my best 'with' mentee."

Annie quickly moved on to a new subject as high school girls are inclined to do, turned her attention to my mom and said, "Gram, you promised you would show me how to make the chicken burrito recipe. When can we do it?"

Mom replied, "Whenever you want, honey. You just have to make sure you cook the chicken enough first. I'll show you how."

"Are you making it for a boy, Annie?" I teased.

"I'm ignoring you, Mom."

A typical night. An ordinary conversation.

But, for me, it really was not so ordinary after all. As I looked around the fire-pit and soaked in that last five-minute sweep of time, I had a little lump in my throat. Here are three generations all connected by a mentoring process that would last a lifetime; it empowered both what we touched today and what we would do tomorrow.

As I looked over at my mother and father, images of Share by Showing memories from my childhood flooded my mind. How did I learn about the cattle business? Rides in the pickup truck through the pastures with my dad. How did I learn to bake the best Italian lasagna outside of Italy? Time in the kitchen with my mom, watching and helping her create her chef-like dinners.

"Lori, come with me and I will show you. Then you can do it too." They said that about hundreds of subjects, hundreds of times.

I looked at my kids and basked in the fact they are learning to pass the learning baton on even now to their friends, to each other.

Hours before I'd heard Andrew say, "Annie, I'm not sure how to take care of my fish so that they will live." (We have had our share of fish casualties at our house.)

"Here, Andrew, make sure you only feed them once a day with three sprinkles, just enough so they can polish it off in about five minutes." He had stood by and observed as she lightly sprinkled the food over the top of the water.

"Now adjust the regulator so it's less bubbly," she continued, "you don't want them to feel like they're in a Jacuzzi tub." He adjusted it under her careful watch and voila, Nemo and Flipper swam gratefully through their renewed fish paradise.

My son looks up to his sister. She teaches him by sharing and showing. And he does the same for her.

Throughout that day, I saw a lifetime of mentoring manifest in a few ordinary conversations.

And better yet, I know that it will multiply into the future.

"I Do" to "You Do."

Know. Show. Grow. Go.

I began this book with a definition of mentoring. You've seen it emanate through the MentorShift techniques, ideas and stories and as you've walked through the Four Steps:

> *Mentoring is a **process** of **mutually sharing your life** with a **chosen person** on a **consistent basis** with the **goal of building them towards maturity in a desired area** and **equipping them to reproduce that process** in someone else.*

It's a longer way of saying…Know. Show. Grow. Go.

Do you recall my words in the opening chapters? I said, "I want to shift your idea of mentoring, shake it up, make your future mentoring experiences a 7.5 on the Richter scale."

- No more sitting in your offices, backsides glued to your swivel chairs.
- No more one-way talk where a mentor talks on and the mentee sleepily receives.
- No more yawner curriculum or "required-read-and-discuss" company-issued books.

Whether in your family or your workplace, you know now to intentionally make the change to a different way of mentoring.

You are in charge. You are the designer of your mentoring relationships.

Through being on the move as you Share by Showing, as you walk through the Four Steps together, as you equip your mentee to become a mentor—you have changed your perspective on mentoring.

Things will never be the same. You have made the shift.

You will make your own "ding in the universe."

Many will remember how Maya Angelou touched the world when she read her poem, "On the Pulse of Morning," at President Bill Clinton's 1993 inauguration.

At 85, Ms. Angelou has had a life of mentoring and has touched the lives of millions who have had joy in reading her works. Ms. Angelou speaks to the role of a mentor in her relatable yet eloquent way:

> "In order to be a mentor, and an effective one, one must care. You must care. You don't have to know how many square miles are in Idaho, you don't need to know what is the chemical makeup…of blood or water. Know what you know and care about the person, care about what you know and care about the person you're sharing with.

> "So if you know how to change a tire and that's all, that's good. **But teach them by showing, by caring that they know these things.** [emphasis mine] Then that will be of use some day. And it may never be actually called out. I don't think I'll be called out to change a tire. But I know fundamentally how to change a tire, and if I physically can't do it, I may be able to attract some young person, and tell him how to take the lugs off…See? So a mentor helps the person to interpret the world."[64]

I feel as if Ms. Angelou had written *MentorShift* with me.

> "But teach them by showing, by caring that they know these things."

That's what I'm talking about.

Know. Show. Grow. Go.
MentorShift.

Appendix

For the Business Leader—
ROI: A Business Case for Mentoring

"In investing, what is comfortable is rarely profitable."
— ROBERT ARNOTT, ENTREPRENEUR AND GLOBAL EQUITY STRATEGIST

Y OU'RE SITTING IN YOUR Financial Strategies class, last period of the day, dreaming of a quick, life-saving trip to Chipotle to fend off starvation. The professor is engaged in a long-winded ramble about financial formulas.

"And the coup-de-grace, the formula-to-beat-all-formulas, is the ROI! What is that, you ask? Your return on investment! I want you all to memorize this fundamental calculation that will help you evaluate the efficiency of your investments for the rest of your business lives.

"This winning formula is derived by taking your gain from your investment minus the cost of your investment, divided by the cost of your investment. And it can be modified to suit any situation, depending on what you consider returns and costs. Beautiful, isn't it?"

"Okay, got it," you think. ("Should I get chips and guac or the burrito bowl?")

Should a professor get this excited about numerators and denominators? Maybe yours did, whether he should or shouldn't have. But one thing he said is true: It's imperative to know and understand your ROI to weigh the goodness of a business investment.

Every company leader, manager and employee worth their salt wants to increase their organization's ROI. Talent development through mentoring should be a clear way to increase company and personal returns.

But you can pick up any business journal and see that companies are in trouble when it comes to developing talent and reducing that one irksome piece of the ROI numerator, the cost of investment.

I began this book with a statistic about the amount companies spent on outside training and development in 2011—a staggering $156 billion. Businesses are investing in developing talent by spending dollars of such magnitude and the money is going largely to outside training consultants.

What are companies hoping to achieve with that investment? Training dollars → More satisfied employees → Reduced turnover → Less cost = a better ROI.

> **Have companies achieved their desired outcome?**

Recent facts on the overall results of those expenditures run along these lines:

- Turnover has not decreased:
  - As determined by Compdata Surveys' BenchmarkPro 2012, the national average total turnover rate for 2011 was 15.2 percent, up 0.8 percent over the prior year. Voluntary turnover rates rose 0.7 points to 9.8 percent during the same period.[65]

- Replacement costs (exit, recruiting, hiring, interviewing, training) still burden the organization:
  - Research suggests that direct replacement costs can reach as high as 50% to 60% of an employee's annual salary, with total costs associated with turnover ranging from 90% to 200% of their total salary.[66]

- 92 out of 96 Fortune 500 CEOs report being interested in the business impact of their company's learning and development programs; however, a mere 8% of respondents say they are currently doing this.[67]

Conclusion: Current strategy is not working.

> **Will formal mentoring programs help?**

Although it's a small percentage of those who can and will quantify the impact, several companies with established formal mentoring programs have measured their economic benefits. For example:

- *Reduced turnover*
  KPMG (a Big Four auditing firm)—Mentees are encouraged to use Dialogue, KPMG's firm-wide, computerized performance management system, to track their mentoring relationships. The firm is able to compare turnover rates of people with mentors to those without to better understand the relationship between mentoring and career development. In 2008, turnover among staff and managers with mentors was 17% to 18% lower than it was for those without mentors. Among partners, those with mentors experienced 50% less turnover than those without.[68]

- *Enhanced Productivity/Employee Retention*
  Sodexo's (a food services company) formal mentoring program, called IMPACT, is tied to ROI results. It is a structured, yearlong initiative designed for mid-level managers and above, including the C-suite level executives who serve as mentors. Sodexo examines ROI directly related to mentoring activities three to six months following the conclusion of an IMPACT cycle, when it gathers qualitative and quantitative feedback from both mentees and mentors. In 2009, the program received an ROI of 2 to 1, which is largely attributable to enhanced productivity and employee retention.[69]

Conclusion: If mentoring programs become culturally accepted and practiced, significant cost reductions can occur.

As we've discussed, formal mentoring programs alone do not necessarily guarantee employee satisfaction and development, but they do take the right step by demonstrating company commitment towards that end.

Measuring mentoring ROI is a tricky business but it can and has been done. Calculating the costs can get pushed off for several reasons: For instance, there may be no process in place to gather the costs or top management isn't fully aware of the costs.

Plus, isn't it the human resource department's job to measure it?

It takes company discipline to categorize the cost and investment dollars to effectively calculate a quantitative ROI.

Back now to our original observation: Companies are sitting on their solution and are not leveraging the power within their ranks to improve their return on investment.

As in the cases of KPMG and Sodexo, quantitatively there is a case for good mentoring. There is an equally compelling qualitative one. Have you read any article recently on employee retention that doesn't cite an effective talent development process as a key to retention?

MentorShift is organically grown from within the company and does not require expensive matching systems or budget-stretching investments in high-dollar consultants. Its key principles make it compelling to any size business—quantitatively and qualitatively.

Beverley Kaye, in her book, *Help Them Grow or Watch Them Go—Career Conversations Employees Want* writes, "Career development is among the most forgotten tools for driving business results...yet is completely within a manager's sphere of influence."[70]

I agree and would add that it is also within the mentor's sphere of influence.

Steve, a lawyer friend of mine from Chicago, used to take great delight in ribbing me about my Midwestern upbringing and life in cattle country as a youth. Steve designed a letterhead with a smiling cow at top center that read, "A Bachman Cow is a Happy Cow." (I always wondered why he didn't have better things to do with his time!)

I think there's a similar letterhead worthy of design—

"A Mentored Employee is a Satisfied Employee."

And that drives a big ROI.

Questions to Motivate MentorShift

1. Does your company quantitatively measure mentoring results? If so, how?

2. How would you measure mentoring ROI qualitatively?

3. Has it been your experience that employees with good mentors are more satisfied in their careers? Explain.

More Questions for the MentorView

For Mentees:
Find a Million-Dollar Mentor by Asking Yourself These
10 Best Questions®
By Dr. Dede Bonner, The Question Doctor
    www.10bestquestions.com

Highlight

Don't just pop the big question to a potential mentor, "Will you be mine?" "Maximize your mentor by thinking before asking," urges Timothy Butler, Director of Harvard Business School's Career Development Programs. Ask yourself these expert-originated questions to better target your mentor search.

The 10 Best Questions®

1. What are the real success factors in my profession or organization?
2. Would I benefit most from a big-picture thinker or an insider to my profession or organization?
3. Do I have access to a formal mentor program or do I prefer the informal route?
4. How committed am I to do the necessary research to find and develop a sustainable relationship with a mentor?
5. Do I really need a mentor? Would my time be better spent with a life coach or even a shrink?
6. What type of mentor do I want?
7. How important is face time versus a virtual relationship to me?
8. Can I handle rejection, risk, and negative feedback from a mentor?

9. Do I have realistic expectations about what a mentor can do for me? What assumptions need a reality check?
10. What should be the critical rules and deal-breakers in this relationship?

The 11th Question™
(Don't forget this must-ask question.)
   What can I give back to my mentor?

....

For Mentees:
How to Adopt a Mentor without Really Asking (But Here Are the 10 Best Questions® Anyway)
By Dr. Dede Bonner, The Question Doctor
   www.10bestquestions.com

Highlight
Do you know what Bill Gates and Luke Skywalker have in common? A great mentor. You can, too, by asking these Best Questions compiled from dozens of experts, seasoned mentors, and experienced protégés.
   The 10 Best Questions®
1. Any thoughts on how to…?
2. Could I share with you how your work (or your success story) has impacted me?
3. What can I do for you?
4. What deliberate steps, if any, have you taken in planning your own career?
5. From your perspective, how can we maximize our time together?
6. What lessons have you learned from past failures?
7. Are there any topics you would rather not discuss?
8. In your opinion, how can I outperform my peers?
9. Realistically, how often are you available to connect with me? What's your preferred method of communication, calls, emails, texts, Skype, or chatting over coffee?
10. What's your version of an ideal mentor-protégé relationship? Where do you see my strengths and growth areas?

The 11th Question™
(Don't forget to ask this "million-dollar" question.)

Could I contact you later to let you know how your suggestions worked out for me?

. . . .

For Mentors:
Make the Most of Mentoring Matches by Asking These 10 Best Questions®
By Dr. Dede Bonner, The Question Doctor
   www.10bestquestions.com

Highlight
Mentoring can be a tricky thing: most people want it, but don't know how to ask for it. If you are contemplating becoming a mentor, avoid selfish timewasters. Ask the right questions to find the right protégé.

The 10 Best Questions®

1. What do you know about me?
2. What are your expectations for this relationship? From me? How can I help you?
3. What are your career visions and aspirations? Your strengths and weaknesses?
4. Where are you now?
5. Who are your heroes and why?
6. Tell me about your failures and how you handled them.
7. What's your level of commitment and interest in working with me?
8. In your opinion, who's in the driver seat of this mentoring relationship?
9. Tell me why you think you are ready for being mentored. Why is this a good time for you?
10. What should be our protocol for meeting? What rules and boundaries are important?

The 11th Question™
(Don't forget this must-ask question.)

Ask yourself: what's my first impression? How's this going to go down?

A - 3

Confidentiality Agreement

Both the mentor and mentee should complete this checklist individually *(check all that apply)*. Then, discuss your answers and come to a consensus about which confidentiality rules will guide your mentoring relationship.

What will remain confidential?
____ Everything
____ Nothing
____ Professional Topics
____ Personal Topics
____ Other: _____

How long will the information remain strictly confidential?
____ Through the duration of our mentoring relationship
____ Even after our mentoring relationship has ended
____ No information in our relationship is confidential
____ Other: _____

When is it OK to breach the confidentiality agreement?
____ When one party gives express permission
____ In case of legal obligation
____ In case of a safety concern
____ During company performance reviews
____ Other: _____

Use this section to address any other concerns you may have regarding confidentiality:

Mentee Signature   Date

Mentor Signature   Date

Our 4 Step Roadmap

Step 1—KNOW. (I Do)

What skills or areas of expertise does the mentor have that would benefit the mentee?

1. _____

2. _____

3. _____

Step 2—SHOW. (I Do, You Contribute)

How can the mentor and mentee actively foster these skills? How can the mentee "roll up their sleeves and get engaged?" (meetings, calls, specific projects, etc.)

1. _____

2. _____

3. _____

4. _____

5. _____

Step 3—GROW. (You Do, I Contribute)

In which of the above listed items will the mentee take a more active leadership role?

1. _____

2. _____

3. _____

Step 4—GO. (You Do)

How will you know when you or your mentee are "ready for launch?"

1. _____

2. _____

Creating Expectations

HAVING CLEAR EXPECTATIONS and guidelines going into a mentoring relationship is key for long-term success. Use this guide with your mentor/mentee to create the parameters of your relationship.

1. What is the best form of communication for both of you?

2. When is the best time to be contacted? (ex. work hours, anytime, mornings, etc.)

3. How often will you meet one-on-one?

4. How often will you interact with other groups/projects (Share by Showing mentoring)?

5. Are there any topics that are off-limits?

6. What other ground rules do you want to establish?

A - 6

Mid-Course Evaluation

USE THIS DOCUMENT TO check-in about halfway through your mentoring relationship. This will help guide honest feedback about the progress and success of the relationship.

Rate your level of agreement:	Never	Sometimes	Usually	Always
We are upholding our confidentiality agreement				
We meet as frequently as we agreed to at the beginning of the relationship				
Our meetings are beneficial and productive				
We have used the "I Do, You Contribute" model during our relationship				
We have used the "You Do, I Contribute" model during our relationship				
Our communications are effective				
I feel I am growing and developing as a result of this relationship				

Rate your level of agreement:	Never	Sometimes	Usually	Always
The benefits of this relationship make it a worthwhile investment of my time				
I would like to continue this relationship				
TOTALS				

Analysis

Which column where most of your answers in? If they were in the Sometimes/Never columns, have an honest conversation about how to improve. If they were in the Usually/Always columns, keep up the good work and focus on continuous improvement.

Activity

For any of the areas where you marked 'Never,' create a specific action item on how to improve that particular aspect of your relationship.

The TorMentors

WHEN YOU ARE LOOKING for the right mentor for you, you may run across some version of the following characters and need a little help working with them.

These are four well-meaning (but occasionally annoying) "TorMentors"... mentors that could possibly hurt more than they help.

You will find Jeb and Sami in the MentorView process again and probably raise an eyebrow, as they do, at their mentor's idiosyncrasies.

Each chapter begins with the MentorView and then gives you a choice to choose for the MentorViewers...Buy In, Buy Time or Bye-Bye. Would you pursue a mentoring relationship with these mentors if it were up to you?

The chapter then goes on to ask the question, "What do you do with a mentor like this?" and offers specific tips and practical advice for gaining the optimum result while engaging with a challenging mentor personality.

You'll see:

- Too much structure (The "By-the-BookMentor")
- Too much debating (The "ArguMentor")
- Too many meetings missed (The "DriveByMentor")
- Too much oversight (The "HoverMentor")

You might elect to never engage past the initial MentorView with these types or you might decide it is worth the effort despite some their idiosyncrasies or difficult habits. You'll find helpful strategies in dealing with each of these TorMentors if you do decide to link up with one.

Mentees, you will certainly recognize some mentors you've known in the portrayals that follow. And mentors, be sure to ask yourselves, "Do I see myself in any of these individuals?"

Have some fun with these characters. Remember, they mean well!

TorMentor #1
A By-the-BookMentor—
She Never Met a Program
She Didn't Like

"Never trust anyone who has not brought a book with them."
— LEMONY SNICKET, CHILDREN'S AUTHOR

by•the•book•mentor

1. A mentor who holds tightly to structure; "flexibility" is a four-letter word
2. A mentor who believes there can never be too many mentoring books, tools, guidelines or program requirements. Everyone knows: Rules are rules!
3. Mentee can be found occasionally dozing over tomes of mentoring curricula

The MentorView

As Jeb enters Betty's office, he sees her at her conference table poring over a 4-inch, three-ring binder entitled, *"Mentoring Regimen for the ACME Company—Commands, Decrees and Edicts for Proper Mentoring."*

As Jeb approaches the conference table, he notices Betty's bookshelves spilling over with mentoring volumes—*Mentoring for Movers and Shakers, Mentoring Do or Die, OCD, Mentoring and Me.*

Betty mutters, "Section 2.2, 'Hold an office meeting twice a month, never miss.' Okay, I got it, Section 2.2. 'Hold an office meeting twice a month, never miss.'"

"Excuse me, Betty, I'm here for our mentoring discussion."

"Oh yes, please have a seat. I see you are here for Section 1.2 in our no-fail mentoring guide, the 'Mentoring Interview.' I just revere this mentoring guide; it tells me every single thing we need to do each time we get together. I affectionately refer to it as 'Betty's Mentoring Markers.' It's my personal mentoring playbook, you know."

"Well, yes," Jeb inserts, "I did want to take some time to get to know you and see if we'd be a good fit for a mentoring relationship. By the way, where did you get that playbook?"

"It came down from on high, you could say. It's right from the fount of mentoring wisdom in our learning department and I drink from it daily. Did you know that it is very useful to memorize the sections by chapter and verse? That way we avoid any missteps."

Jeb glances toward the door, tugging on his tightening collar.

"Now, to get started, we have seven forms to fill out, three signatures to obtain to codify this mentoring relationship and a couple of in-depth homework assignments for you in the interim."

"Hey Betty, not to be rude or anything, but I don't believe we're signed up for all of this yet. I was just hoping to get to know you a little bit."

"Oh, that can happen later, actually. 'Getting to Know Your Mentee' happens in Section 3.1." She smiles sweetly and flips eagerly through the book, looking for the citation.

Jeb scoots his chair closer to the door and begins looking nervously through a desk copy of *How to Become a Mentoring Ninja*.

Buy-In?   ☐
Buy Time?   ☐
Bye-Bye?   ☐

✳   ✳   ✳

What do you do with a By-the-BookMentor?

In a mentoring relationship, what is the right amount of structure? Can there be too much?

I've heard from many attendees in my workshops who are frustrated with rigid programs and formatted rules of mentoring.

Stephanie, a senior analyst from a medical research firm, said, "In our company's program, I was paired up with a mentor. She chose the book to read, questions to answer, forms to fill out and a timeframe to meet. Our mentoring relationship didn't last longer than the assigned time. I was frustrated with having to follow such a fixed set of rules."

Undoubtedly, there are benefits to some structure. Discuss this up front in the MentorView. A contract to set expectations for both mentor and mentee is of real value to set the tone for future meet-ups.

You *both* have to be comfortable with the degree of formality and structure.

A confidentiality agreement, an interim evaluation and an at-complete evaluation are useful to keep communication open and on track. In Appendix A-3–A-6, you will find some helpful examples to use if you desire that structure in your relationship.

A By-the-BookMentor extends beyond these reasonable tools to shape the relationship. She won't budge from the assigned reading. She makes sure every required topic is addressed in every meeting. Meet outside of the office? Never! Protocol is protocol!

Mentee, how much structure do you need and want? Mentor, how much structure are you driving?

In Sections 3–6, "The MentorShift Steps," you will find productive and enjoyable ways to put just the right amount of structure into your mentoring relationship so that it suits both of you.

 Questions to Motivate MentorShift

1. Have you ever had a mentor that was a little too rigid? How did you handle that mentoring relationship?

2. What were the downsides of too much structure? Too little?

3. Are you a person who appreciates strong guidelines or do you prefer to 'free-form' when performing a task?

TorMentor #2

The ArguMentor—
He Thought He was Wrong Once,
But He Was Mistaken

"I argue very well. Ask any of my remaining friends. I can win an argument on any topic, against any opponent. People know this, and steer clear of me at parties. Often, as a sign of their great respect, they don't even invite me."

— DAVE BARRY, HUMORIST

ar•gu•mentor

1. A mentor who says often, "I'd agree with you on that, but then we'd both be wrong!"
2. A mentor who says "Pot-aaa-to" if you say "Pot-ah-to"
3. His mentee can be found buried in a book entitled, "Persuasive Comebacks: Pounce and Pummel with Punchy One-Liners"

The MentorView:

As Jeb waits outside Augie's office, he overhears Augie debating on the phone, "You have a point there but it's a weak one. I've done a lot of research on this topic. Come over to my side of the aisle!"

Brief silence ensues. Jeb can see that Augie's office is filled with high school debate trophies. Augie dusts one off as he continues rattling on.

"What… you have to go? Well, we can continue this discussion soon. Hello…hello?"

"Hmmm, we must have gotten disconnected…" Augie mutters.

Jeb enters and says, "Hello Augie, I'm here for our appointment."

"Excellent, come in. So, Jeb, what are you interested in discussing today? I have a raft of relevant information on a wide range of subjects. I can take you on in any of them."

"Well, I wasn't really wanting to debate anything, I was just hoping to have a discussion about some current job goals."

"Goals? Now there's a noble pursuit, Jeb. Did you know that people generally set goals that are too high and lofty? Data shows that keeping it fluid in your job causes less stress and makes for happier employees."

"Well, I actually do better when I set a target and aim for it," Jeb replies.

"Really? Are you arguing with me? Excellent, I love a good debate! In fact, I call myself the resident D.A. Do you know what that stands for? Devil's Advocate!"

"I get it."

"So, Jeb, let's choose a technology topic. Laptop or tablet—which is best?"

"Well, I use a tablet and really like it." Jeb glances quickly at his watch.

"I'll take the laptop," Augie rejoins. "Those tablets just don't come with a good built-in keypad. A study in *Wired* magazine showed that..."

Jeb interrupts. "Excuse me, Augie, I really didn't come by to argue... so could we move on?"

"Oh Jeb, my friend, I'm not arguing. I'm simply explaining why I'm right."

Jeb squirms and begins tapping his foot.

Augie winks, "Jeb, did you happen to glance around my office? Proud of my high school debate trophies, yes I am!"

"Augie, I think that's great about your high school debate thing and all. By the way, is the men's room just down the hall?"

"Yes, take a quick break and then we'll continue on the pros and cons of laptops versus tablets."

"Sure, Augie, I'll be back shortly. I'll be thinking about some persuasive points for the tablet while I'm gone."

Buy-In?   ☐
Buy Time?   ☐
Bye-Bye?   ☐

* * *

What do you do with an ArguMentor?

Mentee, you want your mind to be open to a mentor's challenges. At the same time, no one wants an Augie. And of course, absolutely no one wants a mentor who is negative and always needing to have the last word.

Tom Kelley, general manager of global design firm IDEO, believes that a "devil's advocate may be the biggest innovation killer in America today." In his book, *The Ten Faces of Innovation*, Kelley states, "…a devil's advocate encourages idea wreckers to assume the most negative possible perspective, one that sees only the downside, the problems, the disasters-in-waiting. Once those floodgates open, they can drown a new initiative in negativity."[20]

While it's important to have an open atmosphere for expressing ideas, you do want really bad ideas put to bed early on. What nobody wants, though, is potentially good ideas squashed by even a well-meaning negative detractor.

What is a mentee's response to an overzealous ArguMentor?

- Discern whether your mentor's arguments are idea-bashing or sincere concern backed by facts
- Ask your mentor for not just the argument but most importantly, ideas for a solution
- Specifically ask your mentor to pose questions to you about your ideas. This reduces the argument effect and encourages you to dig deeper
- Collaborate with your mentor to come up with positive, actionable items related to the issue at hand

If these understandings are in place, one of the most helpful things a mentor can do is offer differing viewpoints and potential alternatives. In fact, your viewpoint as a mentee can be refined and bettered by a constructive devil's advocate.

I experienced this first-hand in a discussion a year ago with Mark Sanborn, business strategist and author of *The Fred Factor*.

I've gone to Mark for book mentoring from the earliest stages of my writing. For *MentorShift*, I began by taking him a draft of my table of contents and a few sample chapters.

I thought my stuff rocked and was ready to soar to book stardom tomorrow.

Mark began our conversation by saying, "I want to tell you that one of my strengths is playing devil's advocate. I feel I can help most by offering you an objective other-side-of-the-coin look at your book idea. Will that work for you?"

I agreed, thinking secretly, "Bring it on, Mark, give me your best shot."

Two hours later I walked to my car with my brain filled to overflowing. There wasn't a stone he'd left unturned, nor an oppositional question he had failed to pose.

"How will you skillfully answer any detractors?"

"What do you want your readers to do as a result of this point?"

"Why would a reader want to do these four steps? What's in it for them?"

He didn't bother with dotting the I's or crossing the T's. He went right to the heart of why I was writing the book and the message I wanted to communicate. He fundamentally challenged every one of my foundations.

Was I disheartened when I left Mark's office? Sure, a little bit. (Remember, I went in thinking Hemingway had met his match.) But mostly I was buoyed up with the questions he'd asked, the possible solutions he'd offered to each challenge and his continual encouragement.

He had an experience base and vantage point that I admired and I took his arguments to heart. He had forced me to argue my case. In defending my ideas, I clarified and refined some of my basic beliefs. My book is a better product because of the rigorous discussion he brought to bear.

Here's my challenge to you: Seek out and listen to the Marks who can deliver arguments to you with class and genuine concern.

Questions to Motivate MentorShift

1. Have you had a mentor who overdid a "devil's advocate" role? If so, what were the results?

2. When is a time that your mentor's argument changed your course of action for the better?

3. Mentors, what methods did you see in Mark's devil's advocate role that you would want to employ?

TorMentor #3
A Drive-ByMentor—
She Was Here a Minute Ago...

"You can pretend to care, but you can't pretend to show up."
— GEORGE L. BELL, PASTOR

drive·by·mentor

1. A mentor who pops in and pops out. Commonly heard words, "Can we reschedule for a later date?" Also known for, "Can we reschedule for an even *later* date?"
2. Mentor speaks to mentee in sound bites, no conversation longer than can be measured in milliseconds
3. Mentee can be found, due to continued appointment rescheduling, developing a close bond with mentor's administrative assistant; with the mentor nowhere to be found, they speak frequently, send holiday cards each year and buy birthday presents for one another's children.

The MentorView:

(Day 1)

"Hello Dayna, it's Sami, I'm calling to schedule a mentoring appointment with you. Would you have some time next week?"

"Hi Sami, I'm *so* excited about this. Why don't we meet in my office at 2 o'clock Friday. I have great plans for us!"

(Day 2)

"Hi Sami, it's Teri, Dayna's admin. I'm sorry Dayna can't make your appointment on Friday. Would you be able to make the second Friday of next month?"

(Second Friday of next month)

"Hi Sami, it's Teri, Dayna's admin. Dayna will be late to your meeting today. You are scheduled for an hour but she will only have 15 minutes. She asked me to tell you she thinks you can make it an incredibly high-quality 15 minutes. She can't wait to get down to some mentoring business."

(First meeting…all 15 minutes of it)

"Hi Dayna, I'm glad we finally got together. I'm hoping we can have some good discussion today about what a mentoring relationship would look like."

"Oh yes, Sami, I've have been thinking about some things we can do to get to know one another."

Dayna glances down at her cell phone. "Oops, sorry about this, I need to send a text back here. Hold on a sec."

Five minutes pass as Dayna furiously types out a text.

"Sorry about that. Now what were we saying?"

"You were telling me you'd been thinking about things we could do together," Sami reminds her.

"Oh, that's right. Why don't you come with me to the project planning meeting next quarter?"

"Next quarter? Isn't that a little long to wait to connect with each other?"

"Hmmm, maybe so. It's just that things get so crazy. Okay, I'll have Teri set up another meeting next week."

(Next week—a few minutes before their scheduled meeting)

Dayna sticks her head in Sami's office and hurriedly says, "Sami, sorry to bail on you again but I have an errand to run. Here's a book one of my employees gave me—look through it and see if it's something we can talk about next time. By the way, how's your career going? See you! Gotta run!"

(Next week)

"Sami, this is Teri, Dayna can't..."

"Wait, Teri, let me guess. Something came up. Maybe she can meet me in March of next year?"

"Well, maybe. Dayna will be out of the country for three months."

"Perfect! Hey Teri, want to grab a cup of coffee? Perhaps you and I could discuss my next career steps!"

Buy-In?   ☐
Buy Time?   ☐
Bye-Bye?   ☐

※   ※   ※

What do you do with a Drive-ByMentor?

This is the opposite of what we encountered with our By-The-BookMentor isn't it?

In a mentoring relationship, what happens when the mentor's participation is less than reliable?

Whereas other TorMentor behavior is a matter of personal style, this mentor can really undermine the mentee's confidence and cause the mentee to feel that she doesn't care.

It's reasonable to have to reschedule an occasional mentoring appointment. But when a mentor repeatedly asks the mentee to adjust their calendar and most every discussion is cut short due to the mentor's competing time priorities, it's time to for a to-the-point conversation.

This can be a difficult discussion to have. The mentor may be much further up the management chain and the mentee may fear offending them. A conversation such as this is appropriate:

> Mentee: "It's a bit frustrating to me because we have had to reschedule our last couple of appointments. (Cite specific dates and times.) I really do look forward to our meetings. Is there

a regular time we could plan that would fit better with your schedule?"

Mentor: "Oh, it just gets crazy with my schedule. I guess we have to keep it really flexible."

Mentee: "It's important to me to get the benefit of your time on a fairly regular basis. Maybe we can add some real synergy if I could go with you to some of your meetings? Then we can accommodate your schedule and I can observe."

This can be an outstanding opportunity for a "share by showng" type of mentoring. If your mentor cannot meet with you because of another competing priority, you may ask, if appropriate, "May I join you?"

Some situations would not allow this (she is going to a high-level meeting on a personnel issue, for instance) but others might be an opportunity (she needed to adjust her staff meeting time, perhaps you could sit in on the meeting).

If you are a mentee who is driven crazy by this kind of inability to stick to a plan, it might be time to exit the relationship. If you can hang in there due to the other things you gain, then you will need to re-adjust your expectation level and roll with the mentor's changing schedule.

Talk to your Drive-ByMentor. An upfront contract, agreed-to check-in points at agreed-to times, and a commitment to openly communicate will guide the direction of your future mentoring meet-ups.

 Questions to Motivate MentorShift

1. Have you ever had a mentor who frequently changed your meeting times? How did you feel?

2. What has worked for you in the past when dealing with a Drive-ByMentor?

3. Is it possible that someone could be a "Drive-ByMentee?" What would you advise the mentor to do if she experiences this with her mentee?

TorMentor #4
A HoverMentor—
Let Him Swoop In and Help...or Not

"Don't smother each other. No one can grow in the shade."
— Leo Buscaglia, motivational speaker

ho•ver•mentor
1. A mentor who believes there's not a mentee problem that can't be fixed with the mentor's own enlightened—and caring—solution
2. A mentor who says, "If you need me, call me anytime. Text me too. My Twitter handle is @hovercover. I'm never far away."
3. Mentee may be found ducking for cover so he doesn't get knocked in the head by the mentor's hovering propeller blade

The MentorView:
Jeb approaches Harry's office for their first meeting. Harry is waiting at the door, anxiously scanning up and down the hall for his arrival.

"Oh good, Jeb, you arrived safely. I was a little worried that you might not find my office. I was about ready to send out the cavalry, as they say!"

"I'm just at the north end of the hall. I'm on time, aren't I?"

"Oh yes, you are, but I'm always on the alert for my kiddos. I guess that's the dad in me! Five of my own, you know!"

"Harry, I'm here today because my boss thought you could offer some ideas on how to write my annual objectives."

"Objectives? I'm your man." Harry pauses and laughs, "You know that saying, 'I'm from the IRS and I'm here to help!' Well, I'll be the helping-est person you know. But to do that, I have to communicate often with you."

As they enter the office, Harry makes a beeline for the white board and begins zealously putting chicken scratches in the blanks on a matrix.

"What's the matrix about?" Jeb asks.

"It's my brains on a board. I keep a running total of communication with my mentees each day. Note the column headers: Phone Calls, Text Messages, Football Pool Invites, Birthday Wishes, Drop-ins. I make a mark each time I check in with one of my mentee kiddos."

Jeb looks skeptically at the board's overcrowded field of scratch marks.

"I have just one little request of you, Jeb. If I mentor you, would you mind wearing this little GPS receiver so I can find you anytime I have some great ideas for you? It will easily fit right on your belt. I wish my own kids would do that."

"I don't think that's necessary, I'm just down the hall."

"Oh, you're an independent one! Mentors and mentees should stay connected. Just a click away, I always say!" Harry chortles.

"So...Harry. Can you help on my objectives?"

"Of course, Jeb, but just know—whatever you need, I'm in your corner! Now, back to those pesky objectives. I have a template you can follow. Or better, I can research some goal-setting articles for you... or just write up a draft for you?"

Jeb leans back, amused.

"Harry, really, I don't need you to do them for me."

"Well, all right then, Jeb, you take a first cut then. In the meantime, will you give some thought to the GPS receiver? It just helps an old dad feel better!"

Buy-In?   ☐
Buy Time?   ☐
Bye-Bye?   ☐

*   *   *

What do you do with a HoverMentor?

You've heard of helicopter parents, haven't you? They are probably every teacher, coach and school administrator's worst nightmare. Why should the kid do the work or play the game when the parent is there to help 24-7, 365?

The HoverMentor is the business version of the helicopter parent.

Mentee, if you are in a mentoring relationship with a HoverMentor now, or are on the brink of entering one because you like everything else about him, here are a few coping strategies:

> Be direct. Talk to him. Give assertive and respectful messaging about the boundaries you desire. He may not be aware of the impact and consequences of his actions.
>
> ("Rich, would you mind if I take the reins on this one? I want to prove to myself that I can independently carry this off. That's how you can help me most.")
>
> Compliment the behavior you desire. When your mentor does give you free rein and backs off, let him know how much you appreciate it and why.
>
> ("Thanks, Rich, it feels great to do this according to the plan I put together. I appreciate your giving me the encouragement and also the space to accomplish this.")
>
> Take the initiative to keep him in the loop. If you reach out to give him an update on a project you're working on, that may scratch the itch for him to be in on it.

Mentor, are you acting like a HoverMentor? A HoverMentor can be tantamount to a micromanager.

Some good questions for you to consider are:

- How often am I checking in on my mentee? (Ask your mentee what they desire. It could be once a week, a couple times a month; check in so that it's valuable to you both.)
- Am I doing work for them that they could be doing themselves?
- Why might I find it necessary to be so involved in keeping them from failing?
- What's the worst that could happen if I take a step back?

In his book, *My Way or the Highway: The Micromanagement Survival Guide* consultant Harry Chambers quotes statistics that are revealing: 66% of people are being or have been micromanaged in the past. Of those, two-thirds say it impacted their productivity and reduced their morale.[23]

Mentor, I know that's the last thing you want to do! You signed up to be a mentor to help increase productivity and boost morale, yes?

So give your mentee some breathing room, some space to fail and hold off on the GPS tracker!

 ## Questions to Motivate MentorShift

1. Have you had a HoverMentor? If so, what strategies worked well (or not so well) in handling the abundance of attention and help?

2. Are there any legitimate reasons why a mentor might be hovering? If so, what might they be?

3. How might you ask your HoverMentor to not hover so much? Try practicing some assertive and respectful messaging.

About the Author

Lori Bachman, Founder and CEO, The MentorShift Group
After a rewarding financial career in the aerospace industry, Lori moved into a second career as an advocate for the importance of mentoring. Through The MentorShift Group, Lori and her team help corporations, associations, government agencies and non-profits tap into, expand and leverage their talent pool.

Through her instructive, inspiring four-step MentorShift process, she guides individuals to greater personal and professional development and leads businesses to improved performance, productivity and profits.

Lori is an internationally respected business consultant, keynote speaker and training workshop leader. Her audiences and clients include:

- Amgen
- Brocade Communications
- Great-West Financial
- CCAI Adoption Services
- Square Two Financial

David B. Morgan, Senior Vice President at Morgan Stanley shares, "I've seen Lori in action. She's a walking, talking role model of why mentoring is important. I am so glad she is dedicating herself to showing organizations how they can raise their morale and improve their workplace culture by instituting effective mentoring practices."

Would you like to prevent brain drain and leverage the talent in your organization? Contact us if you would like to...

- Honor your employees
- Experience expertise and insights by giving them practical ways to pass on what they've learned to others
- Connect team members through a proven process that gives them an opportunity to make a difference for all involved
- Codify workplace knowledge so it can be replicated by others

Lori's services are available via...

- One day workshops
- Corporate and association keynotes
- Conference breakout sessions
- Internal training programs
- Customized consulting

We look forward to hearing from you! You can reach her at www. loribachman.com or bachla11@me.com.

Here's to great mentoring!

Endnotes

1 Miller, L. (2013). ASTD's 2013 State of the Industry Report: Workplace Learning. T+D, 67(1), 40–45.

2 Magee, J. G., & Jr. (n.d.). High Flight—John Gillespie Magee, Jr. *Arlington National Cemetery Website Title Page*. Retrieved July 10, 2013, from http://www.arlingtoncemetery.net/highflig.htm

3 Kessinger, S. (n.d.). Indispensable Man by Saxon White Kessinger. *Inspirational, Motivational, Spiritual, Quotations, Quotes, Hope, Encouragement, Apple Seeds*. Retrieved July 10, 2013, from http://www.appleseeds.org/indispen-man_saxon.htm

4 James, W. (n.d.). Quote Details: William James: The greatest use of…—The Quotations Page. *Quotes and Famous Sayings—The Quotations Page*. Retrieved July 10, 2013, from http://www.quotationspage.com/quote/23543.html

5 mentor. 2013. In Merriam-Webster.com. Retrieved July 10, 2013, from http://www.merriam-webster.com/dictionary/mentor?show=0&t=1392910588

6 Covey, S. R. (1989). Put First Things First. *The seven habits of highly effective people: restoring the character ethic*. New York: Simon and Schuster.

7 Dungy, T., & Whitaker, N. (2010). *The mentor leader*. Carol Stream, Ill.: Tyndale House Publishers.

8 boondoggle. (n.d.). Dictionary.com Unabridged. Retrieved February 20, 2014, from Dictionary.com website: http://dictionary.reference.com/browse/boondoggle

9 Duncan, R. (n.d.). Being Accountable for Accountability. *Duncan Worldwide*. Retrieved July 10, 2013, from www.duncanworldwide.com/wp-content/uploads/2010/07/Client-Being-Accountable-for-Accountability.pdf

10 Ravn, K. (2013, May 25). Don't just sit there. Really. *Los Angeles Times*. Retrieved November 18, 2013, from http://articles.latimes.com/2013/may/25/health/la-he-dont-sit-20130525

[11] http://www.ted.com/talks/steven_johnson_where_good_ideas_come_from.html

[12] Roberts, D., & Hopper, J. (2010, October 21). Standing Question: Could Sitting Too Long At Work Be Dangerous?. *ABC News*. Retrieved November 18, 2013, from http://abcnews.go.com/WN/sitting-long-work-pose-health-danger/story?id=11926874

[13] Ravn, K. (2013, May 25). Don't just sit there. Really. *Los Angeles Times*. Retrieved November 18, 2013, from http://articles.latimes.com/2013/may/25/health/la-he-dont-sit-20130525

[14] Anthony J. D'Angelo Quotes. (n.d.). BrainyQuote. Retrieved July 10, 2013, from http://www.brainyquote.com/quotes/authors/a/anthony_j_dangelo.html

[15] Deveraux, J. (1989). *A knight in shining armor*. New York: Pocket Books.

[16] http://onlinedatingpost.com/archives/2009/06/match-com-success-rates/

[17] Ragins, B., Cotton, J. L., Miller, J.S. (2000). Marginal Mentoring: The Effects of Type of Mentor, Quality of Relationship, and Program Design on Work and Career Attitudes. Academy of Management Journal, 43(6), 1177–1194.

[18] Brian Tracy Quotes. (n.d.). BrainyQuote. Retrieved July 10, 2013, from http://www.brainyquote.com/quotes/authors/b/brian_tracy.html

[19] http://www.ted.com/talks/matt_cutts_try_something_new_for_30_days.html

[20] Kelley, T., & Littman, J. (2005). *The ten faces of innovation: IDEO's strategies for beating the devil's advocate & driving creativity throughout your organization*. New York: Currency/Doubleday.

[21] Crosby, J. (n.d.). Mentoring is a brain to pick, an ear to listen, and a push in the right direction.—John C. Crosby at BrainyQuote. *Famous Quotes at BrainyQuote*. Retrieved July 10, 2013, from http://www.brainyquote.com/quotes/quotes/j/johnccros137546.html

[22] Goman, C. (n.d.). Seven Seconds to Make a First Impression—Forbes. *Information for the World's Business Leaders—Forbes.com*. Retrieved July 10, 2013, from http://www.forbes.com/sites/carolkinseygoman/2011/02/13/seven-seconds-to-make-a-first-impression/

[23] Chambers, H. (2004). *My way or the highway the micromanagement survival guide*. San Francisco: Berrett-Koehler Publishers.

[24] Warren, R. (n.d.). Where will your commitments take you this decade?. *Purpose Driven—Books, Campaigns, Resources*. Retrieved July 10, 2013, from http://purposedriven.com/blogs/dailyhope/index.html?contentid=5587

[25] Four Stages of Learning. (n.d.). *Engrade.* Retrieved July 10, 2013, from https://wikis.engrade.com/fourstages

[26] Gladwell, M. (2000). *The tipping point: how little things can make a big difference.* Boston: Little, Brown.

[27] Slim, P. (2010, August 23). Connectors, Mavens and Salesmen: The secret to your success | Escape From Cubicle Nation. *Escape from Cubicle Nation.* Retrieved July 16, 2013, from http://www.escapefromcubiclenation.com/2010/08/23/connectors-mavens-and-salesmen-the-secret-to-your-success/

[28] Dahl, T. (n.d.). Command Presence. Tor Dahl & Associates Newsletter. Retrieved July 16, 2013 from http://www.tordahl.com/Newsletters/Volume7Issue2.html

[29] Maxwell, J. C. (2008). *Mentoring 101: what every leader needs to know.* Nashville, Tenn.: T. Nelson.

[30] Buckingham, M., & Clifton, D. O. (2001). *Now, discover your strengths.* New York: Free Press.

[31] Rath, T., & Buckingham, M. (2007).*StrengthsFinder 2.0* (New & upgraded ed.). New York: Gallup Press.

[32] Skills Inventory. (n.d.). *SAGE Publications.* Retrieved July 16, 2013, from www.sagepub.com/northouse5e/articles/LQ_CH03.pdf

[33] Shulz, C, (1950–2000). Peanuts

[34] Maxwell, J. C. (2008). *Mentoring 101: what every leader needs to know.* Nashville, Tenn.: T. Nelson.

[35] Jami, C. (2012). *Venus in Arms.* CeateSpace Independent Publishing Platform.

[36] With | Define With at Dictionary.com. (n.d.). *Dictionary.com—Free Online English Dictionary.* Retrieved July 10, 2013, from http://dictionary.reference.com/browse/with?s=t

[37] Wiley, S. (2013). How Is Education Creating Value in Your Firm?. *CPA Practice Management Forum, 9*(5), 9–10.

[38] Sports Commercials: Gatorade's "Be Like Mike." (2011, May 4). *Sports Commercials.* Retrieved July 16, 2013, from http://shortcinemafinal.blogspot.com/2011/05/gatorades-be-like-mike.html

[39] example—definition of example by the Free Online Dictionary, Thesaurus and Encyclopedia. (n.d.). *Dictionary, Encyclopedia and Thesaurus—The Free Dictionary.* Retrieved July 16, 2013, from http://www.thefreedictionary.com/example

[40] Rowling, J. K. (2000). *Harry Potter and the goblet of fire*. New York: Arthur A. Levine Books.

[41] Kelley, B. (n.d.). Phil Mickelson Biography and Golf Career Details. *Golf on About.com—Your Guide to Everything Golf.* Retrieved July 16, 2013, from http://golf.about.com/od/golfersmen/p/phil_mickelson.htm

[42] Zull, James E. (2002). *The Art of Changing the Brain—Enriching the Practice of Teaching by Exploring the Biology of Learning.* Stylus Publishing.

[43] Blakeslee, S. (2006, January 10). Cells That Read Minds—New York Times. *The New York Times—Breaking News, World News & Multimedia*. Retrieved July 16, 2013, from http://www.nytimes.com/2006/01/10/science/10mirr .html?pagewanted=all&_r=0

[44] Ramachandran, V. (n.d.). VS Ramachandran: The neurons that shaped civilization | Video on TED.com. *TED: Ideas worth spreading*. Retrieved July 16, 2013, from http://www.ted.com/talks/vs_ramachandran_the_neurons_that_shaped_ civilization.html

[45] Ramachandran, V. (2005, January 25). NOVA | Mirror Neurons. *PBS: Public Broadcasting Service*. Retrieved July 16, 2013, from http://www.pbs.org/wgbh/ nova/body/mirror-neurons.html

[46] Glaser, D. (2005, January 25). NOVA | Mirror Neurons. *PBS: Public Broadcasting Service*. Retrieved July 16, 2013, from http://www.pbs.org/wgbh/nova/body/ mirror-neurons.html

[47] Gladwell, M. (2008). *Outliers: the story of success*. New York: Little, Brown and Co.

[48] Logli, M. (2011, September 30). Greencastle Banner-Graphic: Local News: Yo-Yo Ma's 50,000 hours of practice pay off at Discourse. *Greencastle Banner-Graphic: Newspaper serving Greencastle and Putnam County, Indiana*. Retrieved July 16, 2013, from http://www.bannergraphic.com/story/1768782.html

[49] http://www.youtube.com/watch?v=C9jghLeYufQ

[50] Sherwood, C. (n.d.). How Does the Human Brain Remember Things? | eHow. *eHow | How to Videos, Articles & More—Discover the expert in you*. Retrieved July 16, 2013, from http://www.ehow.com/how-does_5006337_human-brain-remember-things.html

[51] Hendricks, H. G. (1987). *Teaching to change lives*. Portland, Or.: Multnomah Press.

[52] Morgan-Short K, Finger I, Grey S, Ullman MT (2012) Second Language Processing Shows Increased Native-Like Neural Responses after Months of No Exposure. PLoS ONE 7(3): e32974. doi:10.1371/journal.pone.0032974

[53] http://www.brainyquote.com/quotes/quotes/b/billgates402608.html

[54] Gates, B. (n.d.). Technology is just a tool. In terms of getting the kids working together and motivating...—Bill Gates at BrainyQuote. *Famous Quotes at BrainyQuote.* Retrieved July 10, 2013, from http://www.brainyquote.com/quotes/quotes/b/billgates390682.html

[55] Action Learning at MIT Sloan. (n.d.). *G-Lab Overview.* Retrieved November 18, 2013, from http://mitsloan.mit.edu/actionlearning/labs/g-lab-overview.php

[56] Covey, Steven. The Seven Habits of Highly Effective People Audio Learning System Application Workbook. *Covey Leadership Center.* (1991).

[57] Johnson, C., & Jackson, J. (2010). Learning from Leading. *CIO 23*(10), 10.

[58] Timothy C. Daughtry, Ph.D. and Gary R. Casselman, Ph.D. Quotation. (n.d.) Retrieved February 24, 2014, from http://www.mgmtquotes.com/subject/Criticism/

[59] Sylvestre-Williams, R. (2012, January 30). Why Your Employees Are Leaving—Forbes. *Information for the World's Business Leaders—Forbes.com.* Retrieved July 17, 2013, from http://www.forbes.com/sites/reneesylvestrewilliams/2012/01/30/why-your-employees-are-leaving/

[60] Goodson, S. (2012, March 25). How Do You Change Your Company's Culture? Spark A Movement—Forbes. *Information for the World's Business Leaders—Forbes.com.* Retrieved July 17, 2013, from http://www.forbes.com/sites/marketshare/2012/03/25/how-do-you-change-your-companys-culture-spark-a-movement/

[61] Campbell, R., & Chancy, R. (2009). *Mentor like Jesus.* Nashville, Tenn: B & H.

[62] Maxwell, J. C. (2003). *Equipping 101: what every leader needs to know.* Nashville, Tenn.: Thomas Nelson Publishers.

[63] Who did yoda train. (n.d.). *The Q&A wiki.* Retrieved July 17, 2013, from http://wiki.answers.com/Q/Who_did_yoda_train

[64] Who Mentored Maya Angelou?. (n.d.). *Harvard School of Public Health.* Retrieved July 17, 2013, from http://www.hsph.harvard.edu/chc/wmy/Celebrities/maya_angelou.html

[65] Average Turnover Rates Ticking Upwards. (n.d.). *Jobs, Career and Recruitment Platform. Connecting Recruiters and Job Seekers. Find Recruiting Jobs.* Retrieved July 10, 2013, from http://www.recruiter.com/i/average-turnover-rates-ticking-upwards/

[66] How much does it cost companies to lose employees?—CBS News. (n.d.). *Breaking News Headlines: Business, Entertainment & World News—CBS News*. Retrieved July 10, 2013, from http://www.cbsnews.com/8301-505125_162-57552899/how-much-does-it-cost-companies-to-lose-employees/

[67] Stern, G. M., & contributor. (n.d.). Company training programs: What are they really worth?—Fortune Management.*Fortune Management & Career Blog*. Retrieved July 10, 2013, from http://management.fortune.cnn.com/2011/05/27/company-training-programs-what-are-they-really-worth/

[68] Dinolfo, S., & Nugent, J. (n.d.). Knowledge Center | Catalyst.org.*Catalyst | Catalyst.org*. Retrieved July 10, 2013, from http://www.catalyst.org/knowledge/making-mentoring-work-0

[69] Dinolfo, S.vKnowledge Center | Catalyst.org.*Catalyst | Catalyst.org*. Retrieved July 10, 2013, from http://www.catalyst.org/knowledge/making-mentoring-work-0

[70] Kaye, B. L., & Giulioni, J. W. (2012). *Help them grow or watch them go: career conversations employees want*. San Francisco: Berrett-Koehler Publishers.

Index

CPSIA information can be obtained
at www.ICGtesting.com
Printed in the USA
LVOW01s0224010716
494875LV00021B/258/P